The
Victoria Cross
Raids

Martyn Chorlton

COUNTRYSIDE BOOKS
NEWBURY BERKSHIRE

COUNTRYSIDE BOOKS
3 Catherine Road
Newbury
Berkshire
RG14 7NA

To view our complete range of books, please visit us at
www.countrysidebooks.co.uk

First published 2014
Text © 2014 Martyn Chorlton

940.5449

The cover photograph shows Canadian Warplane Heritage's Avro Lancaster B Mk X, KB726 which is dedicated to the memory of Pilot Officer Andrew Mynarski and is familiarly known as the 'Mynarski Memorial Lancaster'. Photograph by Doug Fisher.

ISBN 978 1 84674 322 1

Produced by The Letterworks Ltd., Reading
Typeset by KT Designs, St Helens
Printed by Berforts Information Press, Oxford

Contents

Contents (cont.)

Introduction

These are the stories of the 23 men who won Britain's highest military accolade for Bomber Command

For Valour

Since the Victoria Cross was first instituted on 29 January 1856, the medal has been awarded 1,357 times, the most recent was gazetted on 22 March 2013, posthumously to Lance Corporal J T D Ashworth for his gallantry in Afghanistan.

Being the youngest of three services it is understandable that fewer VCs have been awarded to airmen of the RFC (Royal Flying Corps), RNAS (Royal Naval Air Service), RAF (Royal Air Force) and FAA (Fleet Air Arm). In fact, just 51 'aerial' VCs were awarded between 1915 and 1946 and out of this small number, 23 were won by men from Bomber Command or credited with flying bomber aircraft. The latter caveat allows me to include the Blenheims of Flying Officer A S K Scarf in the Far East and Wing Commander H G Malcolm in North Africa.

One of the reasons for the relatively high number of VCs awarded to airmen flying in bombers would be the fact that these aircraft had a crew and, if at least one airman survives to tell the story of their plane's demise, or the action it was involved in, then an award can be issued to suit the incident that took place. There must have been hundreds of occasions when actions as equally brave took place, even surpassing those covered in this book, but none of the crew lived to tell the tale. Those airmen who survived their ordeal to receive the greatest accolade Britain could offer were very often unassuming individuals, embarrassed by the media attention showered upon them and expressing a 'just doing my job' attitude. A good example of this actually took place during an investiture at Buckingham Palace when Group Captain Leonard Cheshire said to the King, 'This chap stuck his neck out more than I did!' He was referring to Warrant Officer Norman Jackson who was being awarded the VC during the same ceremony, but the King, taking Cheshire's point, was forced to stick to protocol and award the Group Captain his VC before the Warrant Officer! In fact, Cheshire is the only individual within this book that received the VC for his outstanding operational career, while all the others are for individual acts.

The range of actions within this book begins with the fruitless Battle of France in

Bomber Command – The Victoria Cross Raids

May 1940 through to the final stages of the bomber offensive over Germany in February 1945. Several VC awards came about through volunteering for a particular operation, while others were simply the result of being caught up in the mêlée of unpredictable events which hang over any operation in a bomber from the moment it lifts off the runway to the point it returns.

The very first story covered is that of Garland, Gray and their Air Gunner Reynolds, who volunteered without hesitation to attack a bridge at Veldwezelt. It may not ever have crossed their minds that they would not return from such a raid, their confidence in their own ability to see the job through regardless typified the spirit of virtually all bomber crews during the Second World War. They were completely unaware of how strongly defended the bridges were and were not party to the poor Allied decision that gave the Germans sufficient time to protect them. With the exception of Wing Commander Guy Gibson, who not only helped to pick the men who would take part in Operation *Chastise*, but also helped plan the raid itself, all of the men who were awarded the VC had no control of the situation they found themselves in.

The chapters are laid out in the date order when the action actually happened, not when the VC was awarded or gazetted, as in both latter cases, many of these happened during the post-war period when POWs (Prisoners of War) returned home to tell their stories. For example, Squadron Leader Leonard Trent's experience over Amsterdam in May 1943 was not relayed by him until May 1945 and it was another ten months before the VC was awarded.

Many of the stories covered in this book could easily have ended in a completely different way and it was down to the decisions made by the individuals concerned that dictated whether they would live or die. For example, in the case of Flight Sergeant A L Aaron, if he had just rested following his appalling injuries, he would most likely have survived. His final efforts to help his crew sapped every last ounce of energy from his damaged body. If Flight Sergeant (later Pilot Officer) Middleton had decided to make for Switzerland rather than trying to get his crew back home to England, all would most likely have survived but would have been interned until the end of the war. It was a fighting spirit and determination, 'to get his crew home' which made him choose the much tougher option. Pilot Officer A C Mynarski could have easily vacated his turret and dived straight out of the bomber's rear exit door and survived, but his loyalty to his fellow crewman stopped him in his tracks and his efforts cost him his life, while the man he was trying to save lived.

Out of this small group of 23 airmen, all from a diverse range of backgrounds and varying levels of education, all had one thing in common; a determination to serve their country the best way they could. Whether this be England, Scotland, Australia, Canada, New Zealand or South Africa, they all had one purpose in mind and that was to make the best contribution they could in the fight against Hitler. Not one of them would have embarked on their RAF career with the idea of winning the VC or any other kind of medal; they had all volunteered to become aircrew and they all took part in the Second World War to fight shoulder to shoulder.

Of this small group, thirteen, Aaron, Barton, Bazalgette, Garland, Gray, Malcolm, Manser, Middleton, Mynarski, Palmer, Scarf, Swales and Thompson were awarded the VC posthumously. Three, Gibson, Nettleton and Ward all received their VC in person but were later killed on operations, the former's demise still causes conjecture to this day. The remainder, with the exception of Hannah who passed away in 1947, comprising Cheshire, Edwards, Jackson, Learoyd, Reid and Trent, all passed away between 1982 and 2001. Bravery, driven by total loyalty to their fellow crew members and combined with a sense of duty, are the common denominators in describing these men.

We should never forget the contribution that Bomber Command made during the Second World War, nor criticise those who took part in the bombing, often with clinical precision, with the targets selected for them. The 23 men in this book not only represent the 55,000 men who were killed during Bomber Command operations, but also the hundreds of thousands who survived; we should not forget any of them.

Martyn Chorlton

Carnage over the Albert Canal

Donald Garland and Thomas Gray (12 May 1940)

Brothers in the RAF

From February 1938, 12 Squadron had been equipped with the Fairey Battle light bomber, the first machine to enter operational service with the RAF, powered by a Rolls-Royce Merlin engine. The Battle was, by 1940, desperately out of date. The single engine had to cope with a crew of three, plus a bomb load; it had a .303 defensive machine gun and was no match for the Luftwaffer fighters.

Just three months after 12 Squadron took delivery of its first Battle on 11 February, a new pilot officer by the name of Donald Edward Garland reported for duty at RAF Andover, having just graduated from 2 FTS on 7 May 1938.

The youngest of four brothers who were all destined to join the RAF, Garland was born at Ballincor, County Wicklow in Ireland on 28 June 1918 to Patrick and Winifred Garland, who then moved to East Finchley in Middlesex. Garland received a good education at the Cardinal Vaughan School in Kensington and subsequently applied to join the RAF, treading water as a clerk for an insurance company while his application was processed. At the age of 19, Garland was accepted for a short-term commission on 12 July 1937 and, after initial training, was posted to 3 FTS at Hamble, before the final stages of his training at 2 FTS, Brize Norton. Promoted to flying officer in 1939, Garland was part of 'B' Flight when the call came to head for France in late August 1939.

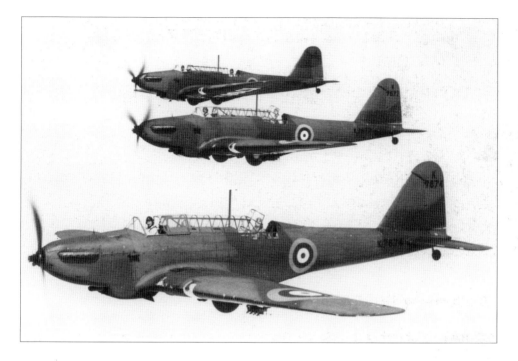

A trio of Fairey Battle Mk I light bombers of 12 Squadron pictured in 1938. Obsolete by the time the aircraft was sent to France in September 1940, the unit re-equipped with the Vickers Wellington in November 1940 at Binbrook, and was destined to remain in Lincolnshire until the 1960s.

A natural gunner and navigator

Serving as part of Garland's crew was Sgt Thomas 'Tom' Gray, who joined the RAF on 27 August 1929 as an apprentice. Training with 20th (Halton) Entry, Gray graduated three years later as an Aero Engine Fitter (II)E.

Born in Urchfront, Wiltshire on 17 May 1914, to Ernest and Susannah Gray, 'Tom' was the fourth of seven brothers, five of whom would join the RAF. Gray's first posting was to 40 Squadron, equipped with the Fairey Gordon and based at Upper Heyford but soon to move to Abingdon. Gray was very keen on flying and it was not long before he volunteered for part-time duties in the role of air gunner. At the time it was not uncommon for this crew position to be filled by ground staff, who were also expected to perform their daily duties. Gray was soon smitten by flying and later became fully qualified as an air gunner, entitling him to wear a brass 'winged' bullet on his sleeve. In 1933 Gray was promoted to Leading Aircraftman (LAC) and by June was posted to 15 Squadron, still at Abingdon, but equipped with the Hawker Hind bomber. Still flying when he could, Gray had to focus on his original ground duties when he was forced to return to Halton for the long Fitter I course, which he did not complete until May 1936. After a spell with 58 Squadron at Driffield, Gray was posted to 12 Squadron in February 1938 and not long after, he was promoted to corporal. His natural bent for flying was clear and his ultimate goal of becoming an air gunner was achieved after he passed a course at 1 Air Observers School, North Coates, qualifying as an Air Observer (later known as a Navigator). During an air firing competition, Gray's skills shone through to earn him a silver .303 bullet prize, and his equally excellent navigational skills saw him promoted to sergeant in January 1939.

A 'phoney' period in France

As part of the Advanced Air Striking Force of the British Expeditionary Force, 12 Squadron was one of the first RAF units in France when it flew its 17 Fairey Battles from Bicester to Berry-au-Bac on 2 September 1939. The following day, war was declared and the squadron settled into the period known as the 'phoney war'. On 17 September, the squadron flew its first operations of the war, which entailed a tentative reconnaissance along the German border. As a harsh winter took hold, 12 Squadron moved to a satellite airfield at Amifontaine, 18 miles north of Reims, from where very few sorties were flown until the end of March when conditions began to improve. It was only from 24 March that reconnaissance operations resumed over German-held territory, but it would still be a few weeks before the 'phoney' made way for the very real.

The pleasant posting overseas for both the British Expeditionary Force and the Advanced Air Striking Force came to an abrupt end on 10 May 1940 when the German forces began their 'blitzkrieg' through the Low Countries. 12 Squadron's war began for real the same day, when four Battles were despatched to bomb an enemy column between Luxembourg and Junglister. No details of success or failure are known, other than that three aircraft failed to return and a fourth was so badly damaged that it was later abandoned at Amifontaine. While the majority of the action involving RAF bombers on the first official day of the Battle of France concentrated on attacking enemy troops on the move and enemy-held airfields, no particular attention was paid to lines of communications, including bridges. As a result, several crucial river crossings, including the metal bridge at Veldwezelt and a concrete bridge at Vroenhoven, both over the Albert Canal west of Maastricht, were seen to be imminently falling into German hands.

A 12 Squadron Battle rear gunner, who also served as the wireless operator, receives an aerial camera. The rear gunner in Plt Off Davey's aircraft at the time of the Albert Canal bridge attack, AC1 G N Patterson, received the DFM, while LAC L R Reynolds, who flew with Garland and Gray, received no such accolade.

'You British are mad'

Surprisingly, considering the massive force that was tearing across Europe only a few miles to the east, 12 Squadron flew no operations on 11 May but from 0400 hrs the following day, eight Battles were prepared at 30 minutes' notice, and four more could be readied within an hour. At 0700 hrs, Operation Order No.2 was received, requesting six volunteer crews to bomb a pair of road bridges over the Albert Canal, west of Maastricht, the very same Veldwezelt and Vroenhoven bridges just referred to. During the briefing when the operation was announced, the entire squadron stepped forward to volunteer, so it was decided to select the six crews that were already detailed on the unit's 'readiness' roster.

The six crews were divided into two sections or flights and were allocated one bridge each. 'A' Flight would be led by FO Thomas, detailed to attack

Plt Off D E Garland '40105', aged 21, along with Sgt 'Tom' Gray was the first recipient of the VC during the Second World War. The medal was collected from Buckingham Palace by his parents in June 1941. Crown Copyright

Vroenhoven, while Garland would lead 'B' Flight to bomb the bridge at Veldwezelt. Thomas decided that the best way to deal with his bridge was to approach high and dive towards the target, while Garland adopted a low level approach. Neither officer had any up-to-date intelligence about defensive positions and they were completely oblivious to the fact that, since capturing the bridges (which were only two miles apart) on 10 May, the Germans had surrounded each with 300 anti-aircraft guns of varying calibres.

The operation did not start well for 12 Squadron because FO Brereton's aircraft (one of Thomas's flight) suffered a wireless transmitter failure and, after quickly changing to a reserve, he found that the bomb rack hydraulic gear was not working

Sgt T Gray '563627', aged 26. He is buried with Garland and Reynolds in the CWGC Heverlee War Cemetery, south of Leuven, 15 miles east of Brussels.
Crown Copyright

either. Now down to five Battles, Thomas took off at 0818 hrs with Plt Off Davey, while Garland led his flight, being flown by Plt Off McIntosh and Sgt Marland, away from Amifontaine at 0822 hrs.

However, preparations had been made to deal with enemy fighters. Eight Hawker Hurricanes of 1 Squadron, out of Berry-au-Bac, led by Sqn Ldr 'Bull' Halahan, flew on ahead of the small Battle formation with the intention of protecting them. However, once over the target, Halahan's pilots were overwhelmed by large numbers of Bf109s of II/Jg27 and they had no hope of covering the Battles as well. Halahan and FO Lewis were both shot down during the intense dogfight but managed to bail out and avoid becoming POWs.

First to attack was FO Thomas flying Battle Mk I, P2332 'F', accompanied by Plt Off Davey in L5241 'G', to be greeted by a wall of flak and numerous enemy fighters. Thomas still managed to drop his bombs on the Vroenhoven bridge, causing some damage, only to be shot down a few seconds later. Thomas managed to force-land to become a POW for the remainder of the war, along with his two crewmen. Davey also managed to deliver his bombs, but with his aircraft already trailing smoke and flame, he gave the order for his two crewmen to bail out. Davey force-landed in France at St Germaincourt while his rear gunner became a POW, the navigator evaded capture and later returned to the squadron.

Garland, in Battle Mk I, P2204 'K', stuck to his low-level plan and approached the Veldwezelt bridge below the cloud base which was at approximately 1,000 ft. The anti-aircraft fire Garland's flight met was even more intense than that received by

Thomas and Davy. Sticking determinedly to the task, Garland began a shallow descent toward the target with Gray lying prone in the belly of the Battle at the bomb aimer's station, known as the well. Despite round after round striking P2204, the bomb load was released and hit the western end of the bridge, just as Garland's aircraft plunged to the ground. There is every chance that Garland, Gray and the little-mentioned rear gunner LAC Reynolds were dead before the aircraft ploughed into the ground, such was the ferocity of the anti-aircraft fire. Just behind Garland's aircraft, Plt Off McIntosh in L5439 'N' was also being hit repeatedly, including a strike in the main fuel tank which set the crippled bomber ablaze. With no choice but to jettison his bombs, McIntosh managed to crash-land his burning plane near Neerharen, where the crew was quickly captured by German soldiers, one of whom said, 'You British are mad. We capture the bridge on early Friday morning. You give us all Friday and Saturday to get our flak guns up in circles all around the bridge, and then on Sunday, when we are ready, you come along with three aircraft and try to blow the thing up!' The last of Garland's flight, Sgt Marland in L5227 'J', managed to slip through the wall of anti-aircraft fire to drop his bombs on target but moments later appeared to succumb to the onslaught. Last spotted in an uncontrollable climb, the Battle stalled, slid onto its back and dived into the ground, killing all three airmen.

When the smoke had cleared and the dust had settled, the Vroenhoven bridge had not been damaged but Garland's target, the metal Veldwezelt bridge, had partly collapsed at the western end and, for the time being, could not be crossed by enemy vehicles. Much of the damage had been attributed to Garland's bombs, although McIntosh's and Marland's bombs could also have been a contributory factor. The bodies of Garland, Gray and Reynolds were buried secretly by the locals who did not reveal the site of the graves to the Allies until late 1944 when the trio were re-interred in the Lanaken cemetery.

All of the men who took part in this raid were incredibly brave and all of them deserved an award of some description; at least the Distinguished Flying Cross for the officers, and the Distinguished Flying Medal for the non-commissioned aircrew. This was the case for Plt Off Davey and his W/T operator, AC1 G N Patterson, who were awarded the DFC and DFM respectively. However, it was Garland and Gray who received the first aerial Victoria Crosses of the Second World War. Garland, for his leadership and Gray for his 'coolness and resource' in navigating the lead aircraft 'under the most difficult conditions in such a manner that the whole formation, although it subsequently suffered heavy losses, was able successfully to attack the target.'* The total absence of an award, or even recognition for his part in the raid,

---

From the citation in The London Gazette, 11 June 1940.

for Reynolds did little to dispel the pre-war myth that air gunners were 'along for the ride' and it is a great shame that this equally brave airman, who lies beside his fellow crew members today in the Heverlee War Cemetery (Collective Grave 6 F.14-16), was not given a posthumous award.

On 13 May 1940 Air Chief Marshal Newall, who was the first commander of 12 Squadron in 1915, sent the following message to his old unit, 'I send my warmest congratulations on the brilliant attack voluntarily carried out by the pilots and crews of 12 Squadron at Maastricht yesterday. As the first commanding officer, I am proud to see the gallant and courageous spirit which exists, and which I know will continue to bring further honour and credit to the squadron.'

The Dortmund-Ems Canal

Roderick 'Babe' Learoyd (12/13 August 1940)

The big man from Folkestone

The majority of men and women who have won high praise for bravery over the years are generally unassuming characters who would not stand out in a crowd. Roderick Alastair Brook Learoyd fitted only half of this description, as his above average stature made him easy to pick out in a crowd and earned him the ironic nickname of 'Babe'. Learoyd was born on 5 February 1913 in Folkestone, the son of Major R B Learoyd of Littlestone, Kent. He was enrolled at Hydreye House Preparatory School at Baldstow in Sussex, then had a spell at Wellington College in Berkshire before rounding off his education at the Chelsea College of Aeronautical and Automobile Engineering.

After leaving the college, Learoyd spent a couple of years working as a fruit farmer in Argentina, and a short time as a motor engineer; a period of his life when his friends described him as 'pottering about'. His life took a new and more disciplined direction when he applied to join the RAF as a pilot. He was accepted in March 1936 for a short-term commission, and carried out his basic training with 3 E&RFTS at Hamble then advanced training at 11 FTS, Wittering, before graduating in December 1936. A posting to 49 Squadron followed at Worthy Down, a unit equipped with the Hawker Hind. On 14 March 1938, the unit moved to Scampton, where in September, along with 83 Squadron who had moved in the same day, 49 Squadron re-equipped with the Handley Page Hampden. Compared to the good but relatively primitive single-engine Hind biplane, the Hampden was complex, cutting-edge technology. Capable of carrying a 4,000 lb bomb load, rather than

510 lb, and 70 mph faster than the Hind, the Hampden was a major advance in the evolution of the bomber. Many months of practice flying would follow but, by the beginning of the Second World War, no experience had been gained in night flying or operating with a full bomb load.

For Learoyd, the war began on the evening of 3 September 1939 when he was part of a nine-strong armed reconnaissance sortie (six from 83 and three from 49 Squadron) led by Flt Lt G Lerwill with the intention of attacking German warships. However, a Dornier Do18 flying-boat was spotted in the distance and all nine aircraft returned to Scampton without incident. Over the coming months, Flt Lt Learoyd took part in a further 23 operations, quickly establishing a reputation as being a cool, calm, completely unflappable pilot who was seemingly oblivious to the most dangerous of situations.

Target Dortmund-Ems Canal

The target selected for the night of 12 August 1940 was code-named M.25 by the senior operations planners but, during the briefing at 1800 hrs for 83 and 49 Squadron the true identity was exposed as the old aqueduct, ** six miles NNE of Münster, where the Dortmund canal is carried over the River Ems. This was the more southerly of two aqueducts. The northern one, a more modern structure, had already been attacked by an earlier RAF raid and, as history would tell, these vital river crossings would be harassed until the end of the war.

The briefing for this raid was incredibly detailed, although RAF Scampton's Operational Records Book only reveals that 11 aircraft were detailed; six from 49 and five from 83 Squadron. However, it is known that four Hampdens would carry out a diversion, two others would bomb an unspecified target and the remaining five would attack the aqueduct with 'canister' type bombs, each fitted with a ten-minute fuse. As a result, only five aircraft would actually attack the main target. Learoyd did not bat an eyelid when he found out that his aircraft would be the last, with each aircraft allocated a specific time to begin their bomb run. He would be flying Hampden Mk I, P4404 'EA-M' which he had nicknamed 'Pinocchio'. The Disney character's image was painted on the port side of the fuselage below the cockpit. His crew for this operation were navigator/bomb-aimer, Plt Off J Lewis, wireless operator/dorsal air gunner, Sgt J Ellis and ventral air gunner, LAC Rich.

At 2000 hrs, Learoyd lifted P4404 off Scampton's main grass runway with orders to be over the aqueduct at exactly 2315 hrs. The flight across the North Sea and on over enemy territory, went without trouble for all eleven Hampdens. As planned,

---

** *Google Earth for old Dortmund-Ems Aqueduct, 52° 2'24.39"N - 7°40'49.18"*

Re-formed with the Hawker Hind at Bircham Newton on 10 February 1939, 49 Squadron later served at Worthy Down before moving to Scampton on 14 March 1938. It was there that the unit re-equipped with the Handley Page Hampden, including these two examples pictured at Scampton in the summer of 1939. (RAF Scampton Museum)

Lewis had navigated 'Pinocchio' to a point a few miles north of the target at 2305 hrs. Below, the first Hampden, P4402, piloted by Sqn Ldr J Pitcairn-Hill, DFC, of 83 Squadron was preparing for his bomb run, levelling out just 100 ft above the surface of the canal. Unbeknown to Learoyd, the rest of the raid was also going as planned; four Hampdens carried out their diversion successfully, while the two remaining aircraft failed to find their primary targets and bombed Texel Island instead. If there were any enemy fighters in the area, they had certainly been distracted from the aqueduct, but this did not solve the problem of the densely packed mobile light flak units which were along each side of the canal. During Pitcairn-Hill's run, the four waiting Hampdens, circling above, were given a colourful display of just how many guns there were, now protecting the aqueduct. Despite being hit several times, P4402 managed to deliver its time-delayed bombs and limp home.

With gun crews well and truly alerted, the next Hampden to attack was 83 Squadron's P4410, flown by FO E H Ross, RAAF, DFC. Within seconds of beginning his bomb run, the Hampden received a direct flak hit, burst into flames and crashed alongside the canal killing all four crew instantly. Third to attack was another Australian, Flt Lt A R Mulligan, DFC in Hampden, P4340 who looked as if he was going to make it, when, at the point of release, the bomber was hit in the port engine, forcing him to jettison his bomb load. Trailing flame, Mulligan managed to harness the momentum of the Hampden to reach 2,000 ft, at which point he ordered his crew to bail out. Once he was sure his crew had left the stricken bomber, Mulligan took to his chute. While it had been thought that all four men survived, two of the crew, Sgts S D Hill and R Abel were killed, while Mulligan and Sgt W G W Younger survived to become POWs. The fourth Hampden to attack was that of Plt Off Matthews. He was lucky to dodge the increasingly accurate multi-calibre flak, and be able to drop his bombs before limping back home on one engine.

'Pinocchio' runs the gauntlet

A lesser man may have been forgiven for doubting the sanity of what he was about to embark upon, but on the outside at least, Learoyd, who had been calmly circling overhead waiting his turn to attack, showed no hesitation.

A mere six minutes had passed when Learoyd began to descend to a height of 300 ft, three miles from the aqueduct. With orders to bomb at 2323 hrs, Learoyd began a shallow dive directly over the canal, well aware that the enemy gunners and searchlight operators had a pretty good idea of the height at which they should expect the Hampden. The previous four aircraft had flown over the water at just 100 ft and whether that was just enough to put off the gunner's aim is not clear, but Learoyd levelled out at 150 ft. On reaching a point just under three quarters of a mile

Flt Lt R A B 'Babe' Learoyd, in full flying gear at Scampton, in 1939.

The cockpit of the Handley Page Hampden was more like that in a fighter aircraft. A big man like Learoyd would have found it cosy to say the least. The Hampden was popular with its pilots and was praised by all for its handling qualities, but it was not the ideal machine for fighting in, especially for the rest of the crew within its narrow fuselage. (Aeroplane)

from the target, 'control' was handed over to Plt Off Lewis. Searchlights coned the bomber and the flak barrage began. As the beams momentarily blinded Learoyd, he bobbed his head down low in the cockpit, putting total faith in his instruments and orders from Lewis.

At least one flak shell went through the starboard wing, almost throwing the Hampden off course and moments later, a second ripped between the starboard engine and the rear of the cockpit. Both air gunners, Ellis and Rich, did their best to shoot out the searchlights, while bullets peppered the underside of their aircraft. Learoyd never flickered during the bomb run, patiently waiting until Lewis uttered the words, 'OK, finish'. On hearing these words, Learoyd pulled back on the yolk and pointed 'Pinocchio' at a piece of sky which was not filled with enemy lead.

Once everything had calmed down, the crew took stock of the situation and began to access the damage that had been caused to 'Pinocchio'. Remarkably, none of the crew had been injured, although Sgt Ellis reported that one of the two carrier pigeons on board had been so overwhelmed by the whole experience that it had laid an egg! The aircraft was a different matter, while the holes were serious, the flak had missed the fuel tanks. It was the shot-out hydraulic system that was the biggest problem, it had resulted in part-extended flaps and no way of determining if the undercarriage was locked down when it came to the crucial landing at Scampton. Both Bristol Pegasus radials were running sweetly, although performance was reduced because of the drooping flaps. Learoyd set a steady course for home and was back over England at 0200 hrs but, on reaching Scampton, which was shrouded in darkness, he decided not to risk landing in such conditions with a damaged aircraft. 'Pinocchio' circled over Scampton until first light and, with no idea as to whether the undercarriage could stand the strain, Learoyd carried out a perfect landing a few minutes after 0500 hrs, without causing injury to his crew, or further damage to the aircraft.

Future leader

Photographs from post-raid reconnaissance showed that the raid was a huge success and barge traffic along the canal was disrupted for at least a month. On 17 August, a Special Order of the Day was presented by Scampton's Station Commander, Gp Capt H S P Walmsley, OBE, MC, DFC stating, 'His Majesty the King has been graciously pleased to confer the Victoria Cross on Acting Flt Lt Roderick Alastair Brook Learoyd (37860) in recognition of most conspicuous bravery.' Sqn Ldr Pitcairn-Hill was awarded the DSO and Mulligan, who was settling down to a long stretch as a POW, was awarded a bar to his DFC.

The Dortmund-Ems raid was, for Learoyd, the culmination of a series of operations, and the VC was really recognition for all of his efforts so far. The attack on the aqueduct was a particularly brave action and going in last – when those before him had stirred up the hornets a little more each time – took a special individual.

Learoyd was awarded the VC at an investiture on 9 September 1940, by which time he had been promoted to squadron leader and was enjoying a period away from operations as Aide de Camp to Air Chief Marshal Sir R Brooke-Popham. Sqn Ldr Learoyd was back on operations from 28 February 1941 when he became Commanding Officer of 83 Squadron, followed by a tour at Cottesmore as an instructor at 14 OTU, from June. In December 1941, Learoyd was on operations again, this time as the CO of 44 (Rhodesia) Squadron at Waddington, the first unit to receive the Avro Lancaster. Further tours of duty followed at 25 OTU, a spell as a PRO then back to flying with 109 and 107 OTUs. Learoyd completed his RAF flying career with 48 Squadron, flying Dakotas out of West Africa and finally 1314 Flight, also flying the Dakota out of Accra. He was demobilised on 14 October 1946 and placed on the reserve as a wing commander.

After leaving the RAF, Learoyd flew with the Malayan Civil Aviation Department as a personal pilot for the governors of Malaya until 1950. He then returned to Britain, took up a position with a tractor and road construction company before joining the Austin Motor Company as export sales manager. 'Babe' Learoyd retired to Rustington in West Sussex where he passed away at the age of 82 on 24 January 1996. His VC is on display in the Lord Ashcroft Gallery at the Imperial War Museum, London.

Inferno over Antwerp

John Hannah
(15/16 September 1940)

In support of 'The Few'

While men of Fighter Command left white contrails over the south-east of England in their epic dogfights against swarms of enemy fighters and bombers, the men of Coastal and Bomber Command were still plying their trade, the latter in an offensive capacity. There is a tendency to tell the history of the RAF during the Second World War in stages, the Battle of Britain being one of them where only 'The Few' seem to get a mention. However, an important contribution towards our victory in the battle, which helped make Hitler decide to abandon Operation *Sea Lion*, were the relentless attacks by Bomber Command on the Wehrmacht's invasion barges. The raid, in which our next recipient of the VC was involved in, is one such action.

Paisley born and bred

Born in Paisley on 27 November 1921, John Hannah was educated at Bankhead Public School in Victoria Drive, and Glasgow Secondary School. On leaving school, John quickly found employment as a shoe salesman, however at the tender age of 17, decided that there was a bigger world to explore out there and joined the RAF. He enrolled on 15 August 1939, signing up for a six-year regular engagement. After carrying out his 'square bashing' at RAF Cardington, Hannah was posted to No.2 Electrical and Wireless Training School at RAF Yatesbury on 14 September, to begin his training as a Wireless Operator.

On successful completion of his course, Hannah was posted to No.4 Bombing and Gunnery School at West Freugh to learn the art of air gunnery, before arriving at 16 OTU at Upper Heyford on 18 May 1940. At the Operational Training Unit, he completed his training as Wireless Operator Air Gunner (WOP/AG) and on 27 May, he was promoted to sergeant. At just 18 years of age, Hannah was posted to 106 Squadron at RAF Thornaby, where he would gain his first experience of flying the Handley Page Hampden on operations. His posting in Yorkshire was destined to be brief and, on 11 August, Hannah was posted south to Lincolnshire, where he joined 83 Squadron, also flying the Hampden, from RAF Scampton.

Maximum effort

The operations of the night of 15 September 1940 were encompassed under the heading of Channel Ports, although the 155 aircraft dispatched by Bomber Command that night were allocated several targets, including a few in Germany. Scampton's contribution to the night's proceedings was 26 aircraft, eleven from 49 Squadron and 15 from 83 Squadron – the latter fielding its biggest force in the war so far. The target was coded as Z.11, in response to a report of a large number of invasion barges concentrated within the Belgian port of Antwerp.

Hannah was crewed for this sortie with Canadian Plt Off C A Connor, Sgt D A E Hayhurst, the navigator bomb-aimer, and Sgt G James, the ventral air gunner. Although not experienced together as a crew, all of the men had seen a fair amount of combat. Hayhurst was on his 39th operation and James already had nine under his belt. Their Hampden Mk I, P1355 had also seen quite a lot of action including as one of the diversionary machines flown by Sqn Ldr J Collier in the Dortmund-Ems aqueduct raid on 12 August 1940. Collier had nicknamed the bomber 'Betty' and this name remained adorned on the side of the fuselage under Connor's charge.

Connor took off from Scampton at 2230 hrs, gradually climbing as he crossed the Lincolnshire coast with the expanse of the North Sea spreading before him under a full moon. Flying north of the Norfolk coast, Connor turned 'Betty' south-east towards the enemy coast which was visible from some distance under the glistening moon.

Shells and shrapnel

Things began to hot up as 'Betty' approached Antwerp, which was a writhing mix of wandering searchlights, tracer fire and flak bursts from all directions. The full moon revealed that the report of a group of invasion barges was indeed correct. Connor commenced his bomb run while flak, increasing in ferocity, burst all around. Just as he was about to commit to his attack, he realised that he was slightly off line and, rather than just dumping his 4,000 lb bomb load and getting out of there, he decided to go around again. Descending to 2,000 ft for his second run, the Hampden began to shake and shudder while shrapnel and light rounds found their mark. A few seconds later, Hayhurst called 'bombs away', but just as Connor was about to pull hard on the yoke to get 'Betty' out of further danger, a single shell slammed into the bomb bay. White hot shrapnel ripped through the bomber, tearing through the port mid-wing section and puncturing the tail boom and fuel tanks in the wings.

Instantaneously, the rear half of the Hampden's fuselage, containing Hannah and James, was engulfed in flames. Fuelled by the slipstream, the fire began to literally cut the rear fuselage apart like an oxyacetylene torch. The ventral gunner, James, had his compartment reduced to liquid metal all around him. With no chance of making it to a safer area, Sgt James had no choice but to take to his parachute through the hole that the fire had created.

Just a few feet above him, John Hannah was having his own troubles; the sight of the floor of his compartment being reduced to a molten mass must have been worrying, especially as it plastered itself onto the rear bulkhead revealing the ground below. Wiring all around him began to spit and burst into flame, while more disconcerting were the spare ammunition drums for his pair of .303 Vickers machine-guns, which were also burning and indiscriminately exploding in all directions.

Hannah kept his head and, in all the chaos, he calmly called on the intercom to his pilot, 'The aircraft is on fire.' Connor replied, 'Is it bad?' Hannah replied in a matter of fact tone, 'Bad, but not too bad.' It was at that point that Connor ordered Hayhurst to leave his position in the nose of the Hampden and go to the rear and check on Hannah and James. After struggling under the pilot's seat to reach the door to the two rear crew members' positions, Hayhurst found that he could not budge it. He peered through the window, could see no sign of James but saw Hannah engulfed in flames. Hayhurst came to the quick conclusion that James was either dead or had already vacated the aircraft and that Hannah was a goner. After making his way forward, Hayhurst quite rightly thought that 'Betty' was a goner too and, presuming Connor would soon follow, decided to bail out.

While Hayhurst was heading for terra firma, Hannah was struggling with his compartment door to gain access to the fire extinguishers behind it. After a huge effort he prised open the door and rather than going for his now smouldering parachute, he picked up the first extinguisher and set about tackling the flames.

The fuselage of the Hampden was only three feet wide. This made any movement by the crew in their full flying kit difficult at the best of times. Within a few minutes,

One of several photos taken of Hampden Mk I, P1355 'Betty' showing how intense the heat was within the three-foot-wide fuselage of the bomber. This view shows the mid-ship door, which Sgt Hayhurst could not open but, through which he saw no sign of Sgt G James, and John Hannah surrounded by flames.
(RAF Scampton Museum)

The exposed ventral gunner's position and the hole through which Sgt James left the aircraft to become a POW for the remainder of the war. (RAF Scampton Museum)

Hannah was beginning to feel the effects of the fumes and heat. He was relieved momentarily by breathing pure oxygen through his face mask but it was not long before Hannah needed some real air so he climbed back into his compartment, opened the perspex cupola and literally stuck his head out into the slipstream. With fresh air back in his lungs, Hannah made for the second extinguisher which he quickly emptied and, with the fire still burning, even tried to beat out the flames with his log book. Live ammunition continued to ping off in unpredictable directions, but Hannah, with his bare hands, simply tackled the problem by throwing the red hot ammunition drums out of the aircraft.

Flames, sparks and more flak

In the cockpit, Connor was still busy trying to avoid the flak, the aircraft proving to be an ideal target, thanks to the flames and sparks pouring out of it. One pilot, by the name of Flt Lt G P Gibson, who was on his first tour of operations with 83

Squadron, described the crippled 'Betty' saying, '...flames and sparks came out like the wrong end of a rocket hanging in the air.'

While Connor had taken notice of Hannah's earlier report on the fire in the rear of the aircraft, it was a little while before the Canadian pilot realised how bad it was, when the flames suddenly began reflecting in his windscreen. The temperature began to rise in the cockpit and Connor felt .303 ammunition intermittently striking the rear of his armoured seat. Regardless, Connor was determined to remove 'Betty' from further danger to give his crew a chance of bailing out as, up to that point, he was unaware that he was already two airmen down.

'The fire is out, sir' were the next words that Connor heard from Hannah, who had been tackling the inferno for ten minutes. Hannah did not venture forward until he was sure that the fire was completely out and when Connor finally laid eyes on him he was shocked by his condition. He was in a terrible state, the exposed parts of face around his flying helmet were black, his eyebrows had gone, his eyes were swollen and his hands were seriously burnt making his tattered flying suit seem academic. Connor asked Hannah to check on Hayhurst and James but he quickly returned and said, 'We're all alone.' Still capable of carrying out his duties, Hannah returned to his charred compartment in the vain hope that his radio had survived. However, the instrument was gutted and the back-up option of dispatching a carrier pigeon was a non-starter, because both poor birds had been roasted alive in their basket. Hannah returned to the front of the aircraft, collected the navigator's maps and settled in for the flight home tucked behind Connor's seat, helping the pilot where he could to get the bomber back home to Scampton.

At 0300 hrs, Connor landed the bedraggled 'Betty' at Scampton and, after taxiing to a halt and climbing out onto the grass, he began to appreciate the amount of damage the Hampden had suffered. Hannah's compartment was a charred mess, while Sgt James' ventral position had been gutted by fire. The tail was peppered with flak holes but the most shocking sight of all which showed how lucky the two airmen were to be back in Lincolnshire, were the fuel tanks in the wings which had been ripped open by flak. How on earth the remaining fuel in these tanks had not ignited, defies belief. 'Betty' had certainly looked after her crew that night.

Rapid recovery and award

Hannah was rushed to Rauceby hospital where he made a quick recovery, on the surface at least. On 27 September a Special Order of the Day by Scampton's Station Commander, Gp Capt H S P Walmsley, OBE, MC, DFC reported the following, 'His Majesty the King has been graciously pleased to confer the Victoria Cross on Sergeant Wireless Operator/Air Gunner, John Hannah (652918) in

Sgt Hannah in good spirits during his swift recovery from his burns, at RAF Rauceby near Sleaford, Lincolnshire. Completed in 1902, Rauceby was taken over by the RAF in 1940 and quickly became a specialist burns unit, practising the early techniques of plastic surgery pioneered by Archibald McIndoe.

recognition of most conspicuous bravery.' Hannah's VC was officially promulgated on 1 October and on the same day a DFC was awarded to Connor, and the DFM to Hayhurst who was by then in captivity. Discharged from hospital on 7 October, Hannah accompanied Connor to Buckingham Palace to receive his award.

Hannah was destined never to return to operational flying; instead he was posted to 14 OTU at Cottesmore on 4 November as an instructor. It was at Cottesmore in January 1941, that John met Janet, who he would later marry and have three daughters with. On 1 April, Hannah was promoted to flight sergeant and on 4 September he was posted again to No.2 Signals School at RAF Yatesbury for further instructor duties. At Yatesbury his health began to fail, undoubtedly as a result of injuries from the burning Hampden and the unseen damage within his body which would have been caused by the toxic fumes and intense heat. After contracting tuberculosis, Hannah was discharged from the RAF in December 1942. Although the full disability pension that he received was appreciated, his poor physical condition meant that he could not gain full-time employment and life was very tough for him and his young family over the following years.

Sadly, Hannah, the youngest airman to receive the VC, passed away in Markfield Sanatorium in Leicester on 9 June 1947. On 6 May 1967, Janet and her three daughters presented John's VC to 83 Squadron on permanent loan. The precious accolade remained at Scampton for many years but, today, can be seen in the RAF Museum at Hendon.

Daylight over Bremen

Hughie Edwards
(4 July 1941)

Leading from the front

Only three Australian airmen won the VC during the Second World War; Hughie Idwal Edwards was the first.

His name could not belie the fact that he was the son of Welsh immigrants who made Fremantle, Western Australia, their home in 1910. Hughie Edwards was born on 1 August 1914 and was educated at White Gum Valley School and then Fremantle High School before starting work in a shipping agent's office. At the age of 20, he joined the local artillery garrison but, by July 1935, he had transferred to the RAAF. Edwards carried out his pilot training at Point Cook, and gained his wings in June 1936. Two months later, he was on the move again, this time to Britain following a transfer to the RAF, where he was commissioned on 21 August and posted to 15 Squadron, Abingdon, flying the Hind. His next posting was to Bicester in March 1937, as adjutant with 90 Squadron. This was the beginning of Edwards' long association with the Blenheim. In August 1938, Edwards was lucky to escape with his life following a Blenheim crash and, after spending nine months in hospital, he returned to flying duties in April 1940.

In February 1941, Edwards found himself on 139 Squadron at Horsham St Faith flying the Blenheim Mk IV on dangerous daylight operations. However, it was to be another short-lived posting as, on 11 May, Edwards was promoted to wing commander and transferred to 105 Squadron at Swanton Morley, also flying the Mk IV. Edwards wasted no time and, leading from the front on 15 June, guided six Blenheims towards a convoy of eight merchant vessels near The Hague.

Approaching at less than 50 ft, Edwards singled out a 4,000 ton ship and, despite relentless enemy fire, pressed home his attack, crippling his quarry in the process. Two weeks later, Edwards was awarded the first of many decorations for his bravery, the DFC. There was much more to come.

Operation *Wreckage*

The inland port of Bremen had been receiving the constant attentions of Bomber Command from the night of 27 June 1941, under the guise of Operation *Wreckage*. On this night, 73 Wellingtons and 35 Whitleys suffered the highest losses so far after encountering 'intense night-fighter attacks' for the first time, but the bombs that they managed to drop appeared to all fall on Hamburg. Blenheims took part in *Wreckage* the following day but all 18 had to turn back because of poor weather. Bremen was attacked again on 29 June. This time, 69 of the 106 bombers that took part claimed to have hit the target. The enemy port was set alight again on the nights of 2 and 3 July but it was a small group of Blenheims, in the broad daylight of 4 July, which were determined to make their mark against this dangerous target.

Wg Cdr Hughie Idwal Edwards VC, DSO, DFC.

This was to be Edwards' 36th operation as he led 15 Blenheims, nine from 105 Squadron and six from 107 Squadron, from Great Massingham towards the highly defended port of Bremen. All were in the air by 0525 hrs as they began the 350-mile journey across the North Sea. Flying in Blenheim Mk IV V6028 'D', Edwards ordered the formation, now down to 12 after three had to return with technical problems, to close into a tight formation and descend to just 50 ft above the waves. The small formation crossed into Germany, south of Cuxhaven, before turning south towards Bremen which, despite being a port, was located 35 miles inland.

*Not much time for the bomb-aimer to hit his target at this height. A bomb-aimer's
view from the nose of a Blenheim Mk IV during the raid on Bremen on
4 July 1941.*

Edwards steered the small force through the outer defences of Bremen, skilfully
avoiding tethered balloon cables and power lines. At this point, Edwards broke radio
silence and, as briefed, the formation was ordered to spread out and attack their
individual targets. It was then every man for himself as they all hoped to make their
escape. This method of attack was designed to get the crews across the target as
quickly as possible before the enemy flak gunners predicted the Blenheims'
positions. The experienced flak crews were firing everything they had at the small
force and, in a short space of time, three Blenheims were shot down, one from 105
Squadron and two from 107 Squadron, including the aircraft of Wg Cdr L V E Petley,
who, like the others, crashed into the target area.

Edwards' own Blenheim was being thrown around by flak but he managed to
focus on his target in the dock area and release his bombs before continuing on at
roof-top height across the city towards the outer suburbs. V6028 was under
constant fire during the 10-minute run and was hit repeatedly by flak in the bomb

bay. At least one shell exploded behind Edwards, seriously wounding his air gunner, Sgt G Quinn, DFM.

Rather than immediately running for home, Edwards turned back towards Bremen to observe the rest of his formation pressing home their attacks. A fourth Blenheim, Z7486, flown by FO M M Lamberts, was trailing smoke and flame as he attempted to clear the port but this was the last anyone saw of the crippled bomber which is presumed to have crashed soon after. Of the surviving eight Blenheims now making their escape, all were suffering from varying degrees of damage. One flew back to Norfolk trailing a length of severed telegraph cable from its wings and tailplane.

Edwards made his escape via Bremerhaven and Wilhelmshaven before flying over Heligoland and then, skimming just above the waves, continued north of the Frisian Islands for 100 miles before turning west towards the Norfolk coast. Edwards' aircraft was the last one back to Swanton Morley and, after his air gunner was carefully removed from his turret using a Coles crane and hurried to the station's medical quarters, the ground crew began to examine the amount of damage that V6028 had sustained. The port wingtip and aileron was missing, the radio had been shattered by a cannon shell, there were telegraph wires wrapped around the tail wheel and the bottom of the fuselage looked like Swiss cheese!

Of those who survived this extraordinarily dangerous operation, four were awarded DFMs, another the

*After a 12-year restoration, the original Bolingbroke Mk IV-T, purchased in 1979
by Graham Warner, is captured above Blenheim Palace in early June 1987.
The aircraft was painted to represent Wg Cdr Hughie Edwards' Mk IV V6028
'GB-B'. (Aeroplane)*

In 1943, Edwards was promoted to acting group captain to serve as station commander at RAF Binbrook where he is pictured chatting to an Australian crew of 460 Squadron (second from right).

DFC and Sgt Quinn gained a bar to his DFM. But the ultimate accolade was bestowed on Wg Cdr Edwards who was awarded the VC for 'the highest possible standard of gallantry and determination'.

Edwards' RAF career continued on an upward spiral and he remained in service until September 1963, by which time he had become Australia's most decorated airman. Air Cdr Sir Hughie Edwards VC, KCMG, CB, DSO, OBE, DFC passed away in New South Wales on 5 August 1982.

Out Onto the Wing

James Ward
(7/8 July 1941)

The boy from Wanganui

Born on **14 June 1919 in Wanganui,** James Allen 'Jimmy' Ward was the son of English parents, devout Baptists who had moved to New Zealand from Coventry a few years earlier. 'Jimmy' was passionate about his homeland, immersing himself in its diverse landscape and culture, which included learning Maori. Never happier than when he was outdoors, Jimmy was a natural at sports, particularly rugby, tennis and swimming. As a young lad, Jimmy was an enthusiastic aero-modeller, a hobby that he continued throughout his school years.

Jimmy's education began at the Wanganui Technical College where he opted for an academic career, being accepted into the Teacher Training College in Wellington. Another future pilot, by the name of Edgar Kain (more familiarly known as 'Cobber' Kain) also passed briefly through the same training college, later going on to achieve great success during the Battle of France, only to die in a needless display of aerobatics over his airfield. Jimmy completed his education at Victoria University College and began his teaching career at Castle Cliff School in Wanganui in 1939. However, the war in Europe was brewing and Jimmy, like so many other young men in New Zealand, volunteered for the RNZAF.

75 (New Zealand) Squadron

Jimmy Ward was selected as a pilot and enlisted on 1 July 1940, beginning his basic training the same day at Levin Initial Training Wing. Flying began on 29 July at No.1 EFTS at Taieri, with more advance training later at Wigram. Jimmy earned his wings on 18 January 1941 and, after being promoted to sergeant, enjoyed a few days' leave before embarking aboard the *Aorangi* which was bound for Canada.

After arriving in Britain in March 1941, Ward was posted to 20 OTU at Lossiemouth before being posted to his first operational unit, 75 (New Zealand) Squadron, stationed at RAF Feltwell. His knowledge of Maori would mean·that he would have recognised the squadron motto, 'Ake Ake Kia Kaha', meaning 'For ever and ever be strong'. This would have struck a chord with the young Kiwi, whose parents had instilled in him the need to carry out his duty and look after those around him; both of which would have been good traits for a future Vickers Wellington captain. 75(NZ) Squadron had only been reformed at Feltwell on 8 April 1940, with the Wellington Mk I, the geodetic creation of Barnes Wallis and one of the early pillars of Bomber Command.

Ward arrived at Feltwell on 13 June 1941, the day before his 22nd birthday, and it was not long before he was detailed as a second pilot to gain experience before he had a crew of his own. Over the coming weeks, Ward flew five operations with experienced Canadian, Sqn Ldr R P Widdowson in Wellington Mk IC, R1457 'P'. However, Widdowson was issued with a new aircraft, L7818, coded 'AA-R' on the 7 July, an aircraft he and his crew only had time to carry out a 15-minute test flight in before the bomber was being prepared for that night's raid.

'Routine' trip to Münster

The night of 7 July 1941 was a reasonably busy one for Bomber Command, with 114 Wellingtons detailed to attack Cologne, 54 Whitleys and 18 Hampdens allocated to Osnabrück, 40 Hampdens heading for Mönchengladbach and 49 Wellingtons ordered to bomb Münster.

Sqn Ldr Widdowson, with Jimmy Ward still as second pilot, would be flying one of ten Wellingtons contributed by 75 (NZ) Squadron for the trip to Münster. Their crew for the operation were New Zealanders, Sgt L A Lawton, the navigator, and Sgt A J R Box, the rear gunner, Sgt W Mason, a Lincolnshire man, was the wireless operator and operating the front turret was Welshman, Sgt T Evans.

Laden with a 4,500 lb bomb load, Widdowson lifted L7818 from Feltwell's grass runway at 2310 hrs, settling the bomber into a steady climb out over East Anglia and the North Sea beyond. The flight to the target was one of the quietest Ward had experienced so far and, apart from a few searchlights and some light flak, the bombing of Münster could only be described as 'routine'. After a successful bomb run, Widdowson made one circuit of the target before setting a course for home.

Ward was standing peering out of the Wellington's astrodrome, keeping a good

*Sgt James Allen Ward VC, RNZAF, standing on the pilot's seat of his 75(NZ)
Squadron at RAF Feltwell, in the summer of 1941.*

look-out all around during the run over the Zuider Zee at 13,000 ft. It was a crisp clear moonlit night and the comforting sight of the Dutch coast was ahead. However, Ward suddenly spotted the tell-tale shape of a Messerschmitt Bf110 night fighter approaching from the port side, which had been stalking the Wellington for several minutes. Ward immediately called on the intercom to warn Widdowson, but the device was faulty and the first sign that the Canadian pilot had of the enemy machine was when its cannon shells began slamming into the bomber. Shells ripped open hydraulic lines causing the bomb bay doors to drop open and the undercarriage to half-extend. Sgt Mason's wireless set was reduced to a twisted, smouldering wreck and all of the crew's communications lines had been cut. Most alarming was the fire in the starboard wing which had taken hold after a fuel line had been ruptured. The escaping fuel fed the five-foot flames which ran over the top of the fabric-covered wing. Red-hot shrapnel rattled around the fuselage but thankfully missed the crew, with the exception of the rear gunner, Sgt A Box, who was wounded in the foot by a small piece.

Widdowson instinctively pushed the nose of the bomber down as the attack began, to dive clear of the enemy predator. Because of the damaged communications lines, the crew were unaware that the 19-year-old rear gunner, Sgt Box, had engaged the Bf110 from almost point-blank range with his four .303 machine guns. As the Bf110 banked away from its initial attack, Box opened fire. The twin-engine fighter rolled onto its back and fell away, trailing smoke and never to be seen again.

Don parachutes

All on board the Wellington were convinced that they would have to bail out, so parachutes were donned as Widdowson adjusted his course to run parallel with the Dutch coast. In response to Widdowson's cry of 'see if you can put out that bloody fire', the crew punched a hole in the side of the fabric-covered fuselage to get better access to the burning wing. Fire extinguishers were tried but the slipstream and the distance to the fire made these ineffective. The crew even tried throwing coffee at the fire which missed but may have at least dampened the surrounding fabric. It was at this point that Widdowson had to make a decision, he shouted, 'What does it look like to you?' Ward calmly replied saying that the fire didn't seem to be gaining at all and that it seemed to be quite steady. This reply made up Widdowson's mind, 'I think we'd prefer a night in the dinghy in the North Sea to ending up in a German prison camp', and with that the Canadian pilot turned the burning bomber north-east towards the English coast.

Pondering the situation, Ward decided to try and improve the odds of the

Wellington getting back to Feltwell. To the astonishment of Sgt Lawton, Ward picked up the cockpit cover canvas and said, 'Think I'll hop out with this.' Ward takes up what happened next in his own words:-

'I had a good look at the fire and I thought there was a sporting chance of reaching it by getting out through the astrodome, then down the side of the fuselage and out on to the wing. Joe, the navigator, said he thought it was crazy. There was a rope there; just the normal length of rope attached to the rubber dinghy to stop it drifting away from the aircraft when it's released on the water. We tied that round my chest, and I climbed up through the astrodome. I still had my parachute on. I wanted to take it off because I thought it would get in the way, but they wouldn't let me. I sat on the edge of the astrodome for a bit with my legs still inside, working out how I was going to do it. Then I reached out with one foot and kicked a hole in the fabric so that I could get my foot into the framework of the plane, and then I punched another hole through the fabric in front of me to get a hand-hold, after which I made further holes and went down the side of the fuselage on to the wing. Joe was holding on to the rope so that I wouldn't sort of drop straight off.

'I went out three or four feet along the wing. The fire was burning up through the wing rather like a big gas jet, and it was blowing back just past my shoulder. I had only one hand to work with getting out, because I was holding on with the other to the cockpit cover. I never realised before how bulky a cockpit cover was. The wind kept catching it and several times nearly blew it away and me with it. I kept bunching it under my arm. Then out it would blow again. All the time, of course, I was lying as flat as I could on the wing, but I couldn't get right down close because of the parachute in front of me on my chest. The wind kept lifting me off the wing. Once it slapped me back on to the fuselage again, but I managed to hang on. The slipstream from the engine made things worse. It was like being in a terrific gale, only much worse than any gale I've ever known in my life.

'I can't explain it, but there was no sort of real sensation of danger out there at all. It was just a matter of doing one thing after another and that's about all there was to it.

'I tried stuffing the cockpit cover down through the hole in the wing on to the pipe where the fire was starting from, but as soon as I took my hand away the terrific draught blew it out again and finally it blew away altogether. The rear gunner told me afterwards that he saw it go sailing past his turret. I just couldn't hold on to it any longer.

'After that there was nothing to do but to get back again. I worked my way back along the wing, and managed to haul myself up on to the top of the fuselage and got to sitting on the edge of the astrodome again. Joe kept the dinghy rope taut all the time, and that helped. By the time I got back I was

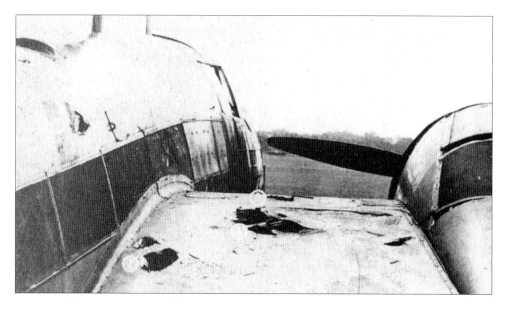

A photograph of L7818 which appeared in the squadron's Operational Records Book clearly show the holes made in the Wellington's fabric by Ward as he inched towards the fire to the left of the starboard engine's nacelle. (Air 27/645 National Archives)

absolutely done in. I got partly back into the astrohatch, but I just couldn't get my right foot inside. I just sort of sat there looking at it until Joe reached out and pulled it in for me. After that, when I got inside, I just fell straight on to the bunk and stayed there for a time.'

Just as the bomber approached the Suffolk coast, the fire suddenly blazed up again as the final remnants of fuel which had pooled on the lower surface of the wing ignited. Luckily the fire quickly burnt itself out and all thoughts now turned to getting the bomber down safely. Widdowson chose to land at the larger airfield at Newmarket, destined to be 75(NZ) Squadron's station from November 1942 to June 1943. The crew hand-pumped the undercarriage down and Widdowson called Newmarket saying 'We've been badly shot up. I hope we shan't mess up your flare-path too badly when we land.' Touching down at 0430 hrs, without flaps or brakes, the bomber covered the large grass airfield quickly before coming to a halt, aided by a barbed-wire fence and a hedge beyond the end of the runway. L7818 was in such a state that the Wellington was declared a write-off, having flown just one operational sortie.

A publicity photograph of Jimmy Ward (centre) and five of his crew at RAF Feltwell in late July 1941.

The crew were whisked off the short distance back to Feltwell where they were debriefed by the Intelligence Officer before heading for their billets.

'Awards recommended'

After receiving a copy of the IO's report, Wg Cdr C E Kay, DFC, of 75(NZ) Squadron, began his regular ritual of summarising the night's operations for official records. After reading the incredible story of what took place only a few hours earlier over the Dutch coast, Kay wrote in the 'Awards Recommended' column of his document, 'Widdowson – DFC, Box – DFM' and without hesitation, 'Ward – VC'. All of Kay's award recommendations were fully approved and Ward's VC was publically announced in *The London Gazette* on 5 August 1941.

A very shy man, Ward found the adulation he received, especially from all who served on the squadron and station, hard to take. Whenever he was pressured into making a speech, Jimmy would always pay tribute to the ground crew or try and deflect attention away from himself.

Now first pilot of his own Wellington, it was particularly tragic that this brave young Kiwi was destined die on the night of 15 September 1941 when his aircraft, Wellington Mk IC, X3205 was hit repeatedly by flak over Hamburg. Sgt James Allen Ward, VC (401793) lies alongside three of his crew in Hamburg Cemetery (5A.A1.9).

Lone Attack on Singora

Arthur Scarf
(9 December 1941)

'Pongo'

Born in Wimbledon on 14 June 1913, Arthur Stewart King Scarf was known to his family as 'John' and, after joining the RAF in January 1936, was called Pongo by his many military friends. Accepted for pilot training, Scarf passed through the Advanced Skills Training at Hamble, then 9 FTS, Thornaby, gaining his wings on 11 October 1936. He was then posted to 9 Squadron at Scampton who were flying the Heyford but, by March 1937, found himself on 61 Squadron at Hemswell flying the Hind. Only a month later, Scarf was posted again to help form a new unit, 62 Squadron, at Abingdon. At first, the new squadron flew the Hind but, after being moved to Cranfield in June 1937, the unit began to re-equip with the Blenheim Mk I.

Posting to the Far East

In August 1939, 62 Squadron was posted to the Far East and Scarf, flying in Blenheim Mk I L1258 with his colleagues, began the long journey via India, eventually arriving at Tengah in Singapore. By early 1941, the allies were becoming concerned about the possibility of Japan entering the war and in February, 62 Squadron was moved north to Alor Star airfield in the Kedah Province of Malaya, only 20 miles from the neutral Siam border. Despite its neutrality, this was the expected route of a future Japanese invasion and 62 Squadron was positioned right in its path. As predicted, the Japanese invasion began on 8 December 1941 on the beach at Kota Bahru on the east coast of Siam (now Malaysia). The RAF reacted quickly but the five squadrons that were ordered to attack the invaders missed the main target because of heavy rainstorms. They did however manage to bomb several enemy barges and landing craft. By noon, Siam had fallen and the Japanese began to bring vast numbers of fighters and bombers into Singora and Patani airfields which meant that the whole of Malaysia and Singapore was within range. At Alor Star, the 62 Squadron Blenheims had just been refuelled and rearmed as 30 Japanese bombers attacked. After the attack, only two Blenheims remained in a flyable condition but through the tireless efforts of the ground crew, a few more were patched up and they were all flown 45 miles south to Butterworth airfield the following day.

Lone attack on Singora

In retaliation for these attacks, the RAF was ordered to bomb the two occupied airfields at Singora and Patani on 9 December. The remnants of the 62 and 34 Squadrons' Blenheims at Tengah were detailed for the operations. 34 Squadron carried out their raid first with just six Blenheims against Patani. A promised fighter escort never materialised and 34 Squadron lost three aircraft while the survivors landed at Butterworth. The second raid, planned for 1700 hrs, was to be a combined 24 and 62 Squadron attack on Singora. The first aircraft away was that of Sqn Ldr Scarf in Blenheim Mk I L1334 'PT-F' with Flt Sgt F Calder flying as navigator and Flt Sgt C Rich in the dorsal turret. Unfortunately, as Scarf circled the airfield waiting for his colleagues to get airborne, a formation of Japanese bombers struck, destroying virtually all of the bombed up Blenheims on the ground. Scarf could do nothing but pray that some of the Blenheims may have escaped the onslaught then, as the minutes passed, he realised that he was alone. Rather than abandoning the mission, rage took over as he thought

FO (later Sqn Ldr) Arthur Stewart King 'Pongo' Scarf.

of his friends being killed. He decided to make the attack on Singora, by then over 30 miles inside Japanese territory, alone.

Scarf kept his bomber low but this did not stop several attacks from Japanese fighters which, with a combination of skilful flying and well-aimed fire from Rich's single .303 Lewis machine gun, they kept at bay. As the Blenheim crossed the

Scarf's aircraft, Bristol Blenheim Mk I, L1334 'PT-F' being rolled out at Tengah in late 1939.

Siamese border, more fighters arrived, but Scarf stuck to the task and attacked Singora in one steady pass while Rich opened fire into lines of Japanese aircraft parked '...like a row of taxis.' Once the bombing run was over, Scarf turned for home, only to run into another dozen enemy fighters who were determined to finish the Blenheim off. Flying at tree top level and jinking between the many limestone outcrops that are unique to the area, Scarf continually managed to shake off each attack while Rich emptied 17 drums of .303 ammunition with short, accurate bursts of fire. The enemy fighters were finding their mark though and, the Blenheim was continually hit by cannon and machine gun fire.

It was only a matter of time before the crew began to soak up some of the enemy fire and it was Scarf, in his unarmoured seat, who was hit the most. A single burst of fire hit the left-handed pilot, shattering his left arm, while further rounds passed through his seat into his back. Seeing Scarf fall forward over the controls, Calder shouted to Rich for help. Rich unhesitatingly left his turret, put his arm across Scarf's chest and held him back in his seat. Scarf remained conscious and continued to steer the damaged bomber on a southerly course while the Japanese fighters left the Blenheim to its fate.

A few minutes later, the crippled Blenheim appeared over Alor Star airfield, where Scarf attempted to land. Near to the airfield was Alor Star Hospital where Scarf's wife Sally worked as an Army Sister so that she could be near to her husband after they had married in April 1941. Meanwhile, with Rich still keeping Scarf upright and Calder helping his pilot to grip the control column, the bomber approached at 300 ft. After lowering the flaps and the undercarriage, the wheels were retracted and the Blenheim belly-landed onto some paddy fields, skimming across the surface until the bomber came to a standstill in two feet of water, just 100 yards from the hospital.

Both Rich and Calder lifted their wounded skipper from the cockpit onto the wing and, despite the air being filled with petrol fumes, promptly lit up cigarettes while a small army of hospital staff made their way towards them. Lifted onto a stretcher and given morphine, Scarf remained conscious and cheerful as he was taken to the hospital. Doctors wanted to operate straight away on Scarf's

Sqn Ldr Scarf's medals on display in the RAF Museum, all awarded posthumously; from left to right, the Victoria Cross, the 1939-1945 Star, the Pacific Star, the Defence Medal and the War Medal 1939-1945.

shattered arm but the brave pilot's loss of blood made a transfusion a higher priority. One of the donors was his wife who walked with her husband as they wheeled him into the operating theatre. Sadly, he died only a few minutes later, his weakened body unable to take any more.

Following the subsequent evacuation of Malaya, all documents and records were destroyed and it was not until 1946 that Scarf's incredible story came to light. On 21 June 1946, 'Pongo' Scarf was awarded a posthumous VC which his wife received on 30 July.

The Lancaster's Baptism of Fire

John Nettleton
(17 April 1942)

From the sea to the sky

Destined for a career in the Royal Navy, John Dering Nettleton was born in Nogoma, Natal, South Africa on 28 June1917. The grandson of Admiral A T D Nettleton, Paymaster-in-Chief of the Royal Navy, John's future was mapped out for him. However, after he finished his education at the Western Province Preparatory School, he failed the entrance exam entrance for the Royal Naval College at Dartmouth. Seemingly undeterred, Nettleton became a cadet on board the South African Training Ship *General Botha*, after which, in 1933, he served as 3rd Officer on the Elder Dempster Canada–South Africa Line merchant ship, the *Mattawin*. After 18 months at sea, Nettleton's career took a different direction when he became an apprentice civil engineer for the Cape Town city council.

Another twist would see Nettleton set his sights on a different military career, quite possibly much to the chagrin of his grandfather. Whilst on holiday with his mother in England, Nettleton decided to join the RAF in the autumn of 1938. After being accepted for pilot training, he found himself on a basic flying course with 8 E&RFTS, Reading, after which he was offered a Short Service Commission. Nettleton was commissioned on 14 December 1938 with orders to report to 12 FTS at Grantham the same day. Two weeks later, he was posted to 11 FTS at Shawbury, where he graduated as a pilot on 22 July 1939. His first operational posting was to 207 Squadron at Cottesmore in Rutland, then flying the Fairey Battle and the Avro Anson. A posting to 98 Squadron at Hucknall, also flying the Battle, followed on 30 September and in November he joined 185 Squadron back at Cottesmore until this

Squadron Leader John Dering Nettleton.

unit was merged in 14 OTU. He remained at the OTU as an instructor until 26 June 1941 when he was transferred to 44 (Rhodesia) Squadron which was equipped with the Hampden, an aircraft that he was very familiar with following his latest tour at Cottesmore.

Lancaster debut

In anticipation of serving with 5 Group, the first prototype Avro Lancaster, BT308, was delivered to the RAF for familiarisation duties from 15 September 1941. Aircrew from 44 Squadron at Waddington, 97 (Straits Settlements) Squadron at Coningsby and 207 Squadron at Bottesford, all had a taste of the Lancaster before production deliveries began. It would have been the aircrew of 44 Squadron that experienced the biggest change because they were operating the Hampden, while 97 and 207 Squadrons, who were equipped with the Manchester, saw little difference, internally at least.

44 Squadron, under Wg Cdr R Learoyd VC, became the first unit to receive the Lancaster when L7537 and L7538 were delivered to Waddington on 24 December 1941. The squadron was declared operational on the Lancaster by the end of February and on 3 March carried out its first operation led by Sqn Ldr John Nettleton in L7546. The task was to use four Lancasters to lay mines in the Heligoland Bight, which they did successfully and all returned safely after the five hour sorties.

Over the coming weeks, 44 Squadron and later 97 Squadron flew several minor operations until mid-April 1942, when rumours were rife around Waddington that 'something was up'. On 14 April, flying Lancaster Mk I, L7578 'KM-B', Nettleton led two one-hour-long daylight flying practices followed by a much grander exercise the following day. Again at the controls of L7578, Nettleton led six Lancasters on a low-level tour of virtually the entire country which lasted for five and half hours and did nothing to dampen 'rumour control'. The same day, completely unbeknown to 44 Squadron, 97 Squadron were carrying out the same exercise. The entire sortie was flown at tree-top level in close formation.

Target for today

On the morning of 17 April 1942, Nettleton and his crew were allocated a brand new Lancaster Mk I, serial number R5508, still coded 'KM-B'. With just enough time to carry out an air test on their new aircraft, the crew returned to hear about their next operational sortie. As the crews entered the briefing room, they were greeted by a scale model of the target which caused many to gasp without fully understanding what was being expected of them. They already had an inkling that their next trip

Nettleton at the controls of Lancaster Mk I, L7578, over Waddington, during training for the Augsburg raid on 14 April 1942.

would be a long one, as flight engineers noted that the aircraft had been filled to the brim with 2,154 gallons of fuel and the armourers had loaded four 1,000 lb bombs, with 11-second-delay fuses, into each Lancaster.

The recently appointed Commander-in-Chief of Bomber Command, Air Marshal Sir Arthur Harris, had been asked to organise a bombing raid against a factory which produced diesel engines for U-boats. The target was the Maschinenfabrik Augsburg Nürnberg AG, located in southern Germany; a distance of over 600 miles direct from Waddington. Those senior officers who had been party to the operation before the briefing began to think that the idea was suicidal, but were made to feel a little easier when they were told that a large diversionary raid would be arranged, and that flak over the target was reported to be non-existent. In order for the raid to be a success, the target would have to be approached in daylight if the navigators were to have any chance of finding this small but important site.

With take-off scheduled for mid-afternoon, eight Lancasters from 44 and 97 Squadrons were prepared for the operation which would be flown at low-level all the way there and back. Only six from each squadron were detailed to take part, the extra pair were there as first reserves in the event of a last minute technical failure.

At 1512 hrs, Nettleton took off from Waddington, followed by six Lancasters from 44 Squadron. The bombers quickly settled into a tight formation which indicated to the seventh Lancaster to take-off that it was not needed for this operation, so it banked away back to Waddington. With Nettleton in the lead, the bombers positioned themselves into a pair of vics and steered a near southerly course bound for the West Sussex coast. It was here, at Selsey Bill to be exact, where the six Lancasters of 44 Squadron met up with the six from 97 Squadron, out of Woodhall Spa, led by Sqn Ldr J S Sherwood DFC in L7573.

From this point, all twelve Lancasters flew at a mere 50 ft across the English Channel, while ahead of them 2 Group began an elaborate diversion raid intended to draw all enemy attention away from the heavy bombers. Nettleton's formation crossed the rising cliffs of the Normandy coast near Étretat, by which time Sherwood's formation was

A contemporary drawing of Nettleton attacking the MAN factory in Augsburg on 17 April 1942

steadily slipping behind, conscious that this long journey would require every drop of fuel if it were to stand any chance of succeeding. The space between the two Lancaster formations would prove to be a blessing, as ahead, Nettleton's group passed close to the Luftwaffe fighter airfield at Beaumont le Roger, 16 miles WNW of Évreux. Home to II/Jg2 'Richthofen' equipped with Bf109 and Fw190 fighters, Nettleton's formation watched as the fighters appeared to be preparing to land after an engagement, with their undercarriages all down. Ironically that engagement involved one of the diversion raids in the Cherbourg area which was meant to keep the fighters away from the Lancasters but had inadvertently led them directly to the bombers.

Caught on the deck

For a few agonising moments, Nettleton's crews thought they had got away with not being seen but it was not to be and in quick succession the German fighters raised their under-carriages and ominously turned directly towards the Lancasters. It was only moments before II/Jg2 covered the distance. W/O J F Beckett in Lancaster Mk I L7565, in the rear vic formation, was the first to come under attack.

A hail of cannon fire quickly followed from Hptm Heine Greisert which sent the bomber crashing into a copse near Le Tilleul-Lambert, nine miles WNW of Évreux, killing all seven instantly. Next was Flt Lt R R Sandford DFC and crew in R5506, who was claimed by Fw Bosseckert. The bomber erupted in a fireball and crashed near Ormes, 8 miles WNW of Évreux. The next victim was W/O H V Crum DFM in L7548 who was attacked by Bf109 'Black 7' piloted by Uffz Pohl. Cannon shells hit the port wing and set it aflame but, determined not to meet the same fate as his colleagues, Crum jettisoned the bomb load and quickly belly-landed the bomber onto the ground near Ormes without injury to his crew. It was little consolation to Crum and his crew, who would spend the rest of the war as POWs, that their demise was the Jg2's 1,000th victory.

The enemy fighters now moved onto Nettleton's formation, still huddled close together, continuing on towards Augsburg many miles distant. L7536, being flown by Sgt G T Rhodes, was the next target for Mjr Walter Oesau, an experienced pilot who had scored 100 victories and was forbidden to fly, but could not resist jumping into the nearest fighter and joining the chase after the bombers. Closing to within 30 ft of the Lancaster, Oesau riddled the bomber's port wing with cannon fire causing both engines to burst into flames. All control of the aircraft was quickly lost and the Lancaster pulled up sharply, stalling and diving near vertically into the ground close to le Vieil-Évreux, three miles ESE of Évreux. It was by pure luck, and the fact that the enemy were by now low on fuel, that Nettleton and FO Garwell DFM in R5510 managed to escape the onslaught, albeit damaged. Sherwood's 97 Squadron crews behind managed to steer clear of the Jg2 and they continued on unhindered to the target.

Running the gauntlet

With the evening then drawing in, Nettleton and Garwell flew directly over the Augsburg factory, dropped their bombs, presumed to be on target and began to change course for the long run home. Unfortunately, Garwell's Lancaster was hit by flak and, like Crum before him he put the bomber down as quickly as possible just over a mile west of Augsburg. Garwell's quick action helped to save the lives of three of his crew, all of whom were destined to become POWs. Nettleton, by then all alone, began the long flight home, the failing light finally affording the crew some protection from prowling night fighters.

Moments later, all six 97 Squadron Lancasters, with Sherwood in the lead began their attack on the factory which could be easily seen as smoke was still rising from the earlier attack. Approaching at little more than roof-top height, the bombers positioned themselves almost in line astern, dropped their bombs and then dipped

777646 SGT. B. D. MOSS. R.A.F.
R64340 F SGT. A. E. ROSS. R.C.A.F.
918988 SGT. B. G. SEAGOE. R.A.F.
1199025 SGT. J.H. HACKETT. R.A.F.
1268146 SGT. R. L. TRUSTAM. R.A.F.
42580 F LT. R. R. SANDFORD. R.A.F.
80067 P O. H. A. P. PEALL. R.A.F.
932122 SGT. G.W. J.HADGRAFT. R.A.F.
777701 SGT. P.J. VENTNER. R.A.F.
962127 SGT. R. E. WING. R.A.F.
17. 4. 42

Both W/O Beckett's and Flt Lt Sandford's crews were buried by the French in a mass grave at Beaumont-le-Roger where they remain to this day. Not all of the crew's names are visible. W/O J F Beckett and his rear gunner Sgt A Harrison are missing, as are FO A Gerrie and Flt Sgt L Law, from Sandford's crew.

even lower in an effort to get under the flak. Sherwood's aircraft took a direct hit and crash-landed on the edge of town. Six of the crew were killed in the ensuing crash but Sherwood was ejected through the canopy and survived to become a POW. As the second vic formation approached the target, R5513, being flown by W/O Mycock DFC, was hit, burst into flames, then crashed into the target area with no hope for the crew. FO Deverill was also hit in one engine but managed to complete his bomb run and turn away from the increasingly 'hot' target. Sporting a ten-foot-long hole in the side of its fuselage, Deverill managed to limp his aircraft home to Woodhall Spa, accompanied by the other three 97 Squadron survivors, none of whom escaped without some degree of flak damage.

For Nettleton, the flight home was longer than planned because the bomber landed at Squire's Gate near Blackpool at 0100 hrs on 18 April. He immediately phoned Waddington to deliver a preliminary report of the raid and make enquiries about casualties. No figures would have been given to Nettleton over the phone at the time but the final grim statistics equated to 49 missing aircrew from seven aircraft. Because of the high casualty figures, this type of operation was never repeated.

Postscript

There was a great deal of dissatisfaction, at the most senior level, with Harris's choice of target immediately after the raid. In a debate which involved Winston Churchill, the Ministry of Economic Warfare was unhappy that a more vital target had not been selected in southern Germany, and they made their complaints very clear in a period of intense correspondence with the Air Ministry and Bomber Command. Harris had seriously considered an attack on the ball-bearing factories at Schweinfurt but chose Augsburg instead for tactical reasons and fervently defended his decision.

This discussion meant nothing to the many dead, and those in captivity following this operation, but those who made it back received a number of DFCs, DFMs, and a DSO. The ultimate accolade, the VC, was awarded to Nettleton for his leadership of the raid. The raid itself was manna from heaven for the press, who boldly described the terrific destruction caused to the factory. Post-war German records revealed that, in reality, seventeen 1,000 lb bombs struck the engine plant, five of which failed to explode. Everyone involved in this incredible display of flying skill, accurate navigation and determination deserved a much better result for their efforts.

For Nettleton, there was a six-week tour of the USA, carrying out lectures and visits before returning back to Waddington. He married Section Officer Betty

Sqn Ldr John Nettleton VC with his bride, Section Officer Betty née Havelock, at their wedding reception on 1 July 1942. Just over twelve months later, Nettleton and his crew failed to return from a raid on Turin on 12 July 1943.

Havelock, WAAF, in Lincoln on 17 July 1942 and was then posted to 44 Conversion Flight, still at Waddington. 44 CF became part of 1651 Heavy Conversion Unit in November 1942 but, still entrenched in Lincolnshire, Nettleton was promoted to wing commander and, on 4 January 1943 became OC 44 Squadron. While leading from the front on the night of 12 July 1943 in Lancaster Mk I, ED331 out of Dunholme Lodge, Nettleton's aircraft was presumed to have been attacked by a night fighter en route to Turin. The bomber came down off the Brest peninsular with the loss of all eight crew who, today, are commemorated on the Runnymede Memorial.

Cologne Raid in 'D' for Dog

Leslie Manser
(31 May 1942)

Determined to join the war

Leslie Thomas Manser, the son of civil engineer T J S Manser, was born on 11 May 1922 in New Delhi. Initially educated at the Victoria Boys' School at Kurseong, he later came to England where he settled with his family in Radlett. It was from this Hertfordshire village that young Leslie was educated at St Faith's School, Cambridge and Cox's House, Aldenham, by which time, the Second World War had already begun. At the tender age of 17, Manser was determined to join the war and straight after leaving school he applied to the Army and the Royal Navy, but was turned down by both services. Manser did not give up and decided to give the RAF a go. They accepted the young man as a potential pilot on 14 August 1940.

With his basic training under his belt, Manser was commissioned on 6 May 1941 and posted on 12 May to 2 School of Air Navigation at Cranage. Operational training was carried out at 14 OTU, Cottesmore, on the Handley Page Hampden, and was followed by a posting to his first front-line unit, 50 Squadron, stationed at Swinderby on 27 August. Within 48 hours, Manser joined Plt Off Ford as second pilot on his first operation to Frankfurt, an unsuccessful raid that saw one Hampden fail to return and another crash at Bassingham. Both of them were from 50 Squadron.

Over the next eight weeks, Manser only took part in six further operations before he was posted, unhappily, to 25 OTU at Finningley on 7 November 1941 and then back to 14 OTU, this time as an instructor, on 9 December. Being very keen to get back to his own unit and a return to operations, Manser found himself being posted to 420 (Snowy Owl) Squadron at Waddington on 21 March 1942. Still unhappy, Manser continued his efforts to return to 50 Squadron which were finally rewarded on 3 April when he rejoined his old unit which was, by then, stationed at Skellingthorpe. Manser also found the squadron going through the painful process of converting from the Hampden.

Disappointing conversion to the Manchester

50 Squadron prepared for an exciting new replacement for the Hampden, the infamous Avro Manchester. The Manchester promised greater range, a larger bomb load, more defensive armament and more comfortable and practical crew positions. In reality, the aircraft was tragically let down by completely inadequate Rolls-Royce Vulture engines which barely dragged the aircraft off the runway and gave crews little chance of making it home on a single engine.

50 Squadron carried out its first Manchester operation on 8 April, Manser taking part in a *Nickel* to Paris. Manser carried out five more operational sorties during April and May, quickly gaining experience on the Manchester and becoming familiar with just about all the bomber's foibles and quirks, mixed with an array of technical problems and failures along the way.

Manser was promoted to Flying Officer on 6 May, by which time he was already gaining a reputation as one of the more competent captains on the squadron, and he was certainly well-respected by his crew. As the end of the month approached, 'rumour control' at Skellingthorpe began to work overtime, suggesting that something different was in the pipeline. On 30 May, 15 crews were selected for the night's

Flying Officer Leslie Thomas Manser.

Photographs of 50 Squadron Manchesters are rare as the unit only operated the type between April and June 1942 before re-equipping with the Lancaster. This is Mk I, L7476 'VN-Z'. Manser's aircraft carried the 106 Squadron code 'ZN' for his final operation.

operation. Manser's crew and one other would fly as reserves. By then, the target would have been revealed as Cologne – not significant in its own right, but 50 Squadron would be taking part in the first of Harris's '1,000-bomber' raids. These attacks were designed to demonstrate that Bomber Command was a war-changing force to be reckoned with, because staff at senior levels had doubted its effectiveness and value right from the beginning of the war.

While their colleagues were being briefed on the night's proceedings, Manser and another squadron pilot were ordered to go to Coningsby to collect a pair of ex-106 Squadron Manchesters, as that unit was converting to the Lancaster. Incidentally, 50 Squadron's own Conversion Flight had already received a pair of Lancasters for familiarisation training on 16 May, indicating that the new larger bomber would be appearing in numbers at Skellingthorpe soon.

Manser collected Manchester Mk I, L7301, 'ZN-D' as instructed, from Coningsby, an aircraft that was not in particularly good order but, after an air test, was declared 'airworthy' and as such was added to the list of aircraft that would attack Cologne that night. First delivered to 27 MU at Shawbury on 12 December 1940, L7301 was not delivered to 106 Squadron until 28 April 1942 and as a result had only flown one operation before Manser collected it, spending most of its short existence with 106 Squadron Conversion Flight. Its performance gave the impression of a machine which had already had a tough life.

'D' for Dog, a reluctant participant

Manser and his crew, Sgt L H Baveystock, the co-pilot, Plt Off R J Barnes, bomb-aimer, Plt Off R M Horsley, wireless operator, Sgt S E King mid-upper air gunner, Sgt A McF Mills front air gunner and Sgt B W Naylor rear gunner, were driven out to the 106 Squadron-coded 'D' for Dog in the fading light. With a load of 1,260 incendiary bombs (IB), Manser started the bomber's twin Vultures, took his turn to taxi to the main runway and lifted away from Skellingthorpe at 2301 hrs. It was his fourteenth operation. As Manser steadily climbed over the North Sea, the reluctant 'D' for Dog's engines began to overheat above 7,000 ft. The aircraft needed to be at 17,000 ft over the target. The thought of being so low over a well-defended target would have made the majority of pilots turn for home, and no-one would have criticised them for it. However, Manser decided that they stood just as good a chance as anyone on the operation, because the bulk of the flak would be aimed at the much higher flying aircraft; a dangerous but logical theory.

Manser's logic did not play out well as 'D' for Dog approached Cologne's myriad of sweeping searchlights, each of them with innumerable anti-aircraft guns in support. As the aircraft began its bomb run, the first of several searchlights picked out the unfortunate Manchester which was followed by the inevitable clatter and rattle as flak shells burst closer and closer to the bomber. With no attempt to carry out evasive action, Manser held the Manchester steady until Barnes shouted 'bombs gone'. 5,000 lbs lighter, 'D' for Dog only felt sprightly for a few seconds as Manser tried to gain height away from the onslaught. However, a single flak shell found its mark, slamming into the rear section of the bomb bay, the subsequent explosion littering the wings and fuselage with hot shards of shrapnel. The blast of the flak had ripped the control column from Manser's grip but within seconds, he was composed again. Pushing the column hard forward, Manser did everything he could to get 'D' for Dog away from the flak and searchlights, but before the bomber could escape, a wall of 20 mm cannon fire had to be endured before the aircraft levelled out, a mere 800 ft above the ground. It was time to consolidate the situation as the crew, in turn, updated Manser on the state of the aircraft which was on fire in the rear fuselage and was filling with smoke. The rear gunner, Sgt Naylor, had been wounded, while Plt Off Horsley and Sgt Baveystock made sure that no IBs were left in the bomb bay, to fuel the fire.

Optimistic course

Somehow, Manser managed to coax 'D' for Dog back up to 2,000 ft which was the final straw for the port Vulture which let go in spectacular fashion by bursting into flames that leapt along almost the entire span of the wing. Prior to the engine failure, the bomber was already proving difficult to handle but Manser kept the aircraft under control, simultaneously ordering Baveystock to feather the port propeller and activate the internal fire extinguisher. Mesmerised by the flames, both pilot and co-pilot calmly watched as the fire burned on ferociously and then miraculously burned itself out. With no chance of reaching Skellingthorpe, Manser decided to make for the emergency airfield at Manston. To stand any chance of reaching Manston, he ordered his crew to throw out as many removable items as possible, the majority of which disappeared down the bomber's flare chute.

With the Manchester's notorious single-engine performance the only chance the bomber had of reaching England was by gaining altitude. Manser did his best to maintain a reasonable height for as long as he could but, with the bomber on the verge of stalling, he made the wise decision to order his crew to prepare to bail out. Sgt Mills evacuated rapidly through the forward escape hatch, while Plt Off Horsley helped the injured Sgt Naylor out of his turret; both airmen jumped out of the main door in the rear fuselage. Plt Off Barnes and Sgt King jumped safely, leaving just Manser and Baveystock in the cockpit. Having attached his own chute, Baveystock attempted to attach a parachute to Manser's chest harness. Manser was fully aware that the bomber was only seconds away from oblivion but the brave pilot waved his co-pilot away and said, 'For god's sake, get out!'

With the bomber shaking violently, Baveystock made his escape through the forward hatch and, within seconds, before his chute had a chance to fully deploy, the co-pilot was on the ground, albeit in a dyke filled with five feet of water, which undoubtedly saved his life. Above him, the crippled 'D' for Dog, rolled onto its back and plunged into the ground only yards away, taking the life of Leslie Manser with it. Those vital seconds, when Manser remained at the controls, in the knowledge that he had no chance of survival, saved the lives of his entire crew.

Evasion and accolade

The Manchester had crashed at 0200 hrs into the same dyke that Baveystock found himself in, three miles east of Bree in Belgium, not far from the Dutch border. All six of Manser's crew bailed out safely but Plt Off Barnes was injured on landing and subsequently became a POW. For the remainder, they were quickly squirrelled away by several brave villagers and, within 48 hours, were being secreted in Liege. Over

The shattered remains of L7301 in which FO Leslie Manser perished on 31 May 1942.

the coming weeks, Baveystock, Horsley, King, Mills and Naylor reached Gibraltar, via Brussels, Paris and St Jean de Luz. All of them arrived back safely in England in early October. It was then that the story of Manser's heroism was revealed and, on 20 October 1942 he was awarded a posthumous VC.

The award was presented to the Manser family at Buckingham Palace on 3 March 1943. However, the family decided to loan the precious medal to 50 Squadron, which was serving at Waddington at the time, during a ceremony on 31 May 1965, thirteen years to the day after Manser's brave action. Presented to Wg Cdr W J Stacey, the medal can be seen in the Lord Ashcroft Gallery at the Imperial War Museum.

Leslie Manser VC was laid to rest in Heverlee Cemetery (7.G.1) and, in recognition of his bravery, an extension of Birchwood Middle School, Skellingthorpe was built

Flt Lt Robert Horsley after receiving the DFC at Buckingham Palace, with his proud wife and mother. Having served as part of Manser's crew as the wireless operator, Horsley trained as a pilot and later served with 617 Squadron.
Crown Copyright

in 1980 and dedicated on 28 April 1981. A second memorial, close to 'D' for Dog's crash site at the 'Zig', Stamprooierbroke near Molenbeersel (51° 9'36.32"N, 5°43'11.54"E), Belgium, was dedicated on 31 May 2004.

9

The Faithful Crew

Rawdon Middleton
(29 November 1942)

The jackeroo from Sydney

The Middleton family first arrived in Australia from Cambridge during the early 19th century. They were led by the Reverend G A Middleton, nearly 100 years before the birth of Rawdon Hume Middleton on 22 July 1916 in Waverley, Sydney. Rawdon's father, Francis Rawdon Hume Middleton, was a sheep farmer and Rawdon attended a number of schools, including the Gilgandra and Dubbo High Schools. When Francis became the manager of a farm at Yarrabandai, Rawdon became a jackeroo (a trainee sheep farm worker), learning the trade from his father. A keen sportsman, Rawdon was up for any kind of outdoor sport, although it was rugby, cricket and tennis that he was particularly keen on.

Like many young Australians, Middleton decided that he wanted to join the fight against Hitler and on 14 October 1940, he was accepted into the RAAF. After completing his basic training at 2 ITS at Bradfield Park, Rawdon, known from then on as 'Ron' in RAF circles, was filtered out for pilot training and posted to 5 EFTS at Narromine. Rounding off his flying training in Canada, where he earned his wings on 6 June 1941, Middleton then sailed to England to join 23 OTU at Pershore on 7 October. His operational training complete, Middleton was then posted to his first unit, 7 Squadron at Oakington, on 6 December.

Cutting his teeth on the Stirling

7 Squadron was the first operational unit to receive the four-engine Short Stirling in

Flt Sgt Rawdon Hulme 'Ron' Middleton came from a strong Australian line which included the colonial explorer, Hamilton Hulme, his great uncle.

August 1940 and from then on was at the forefront of Bomber Command operations. Middleton's time at Oakington was destined to be brief as he was detached to Waterbeach for a month, presumably to 26 Conversion Flight which was formed from 7 Squadron personnel on 5 October 1941. 26 CF was disbanded into 1651 Heavy Conversion Unit on 1 January 1942, from where Middleton was posted to 149 (East Squadron) stationed at Mildenhall on 26 February. During conversion from the Wellington to the Stirling, 149 Squadron established a Stirling detachment at nearby Lakenheath and it was from there that Middleton's operational flying career finally began.

On 6 April, 149 Squadron moved out of Mildenhall to Lakenheath and, up to this date, Middleton had been building experience as a second pilot to Flt Lt M E Evans in Stirling Mk I, N3726. That night, 19 of the 149 Squadron Stirlings took part in a 157-aircraft-strong raid to Essen which was disrupted by severe storms, icing and cloud over the target. However, before N3726 reached the target, it was attacked by a Bf110 night fighter over Holland which knocked out one of the starboard engines and caused considerable damage to the wing. Evans turned back to Lakenheath but unbeknown to the crew, the undercarriage hydraulic lines had been ruptured and, on touching down at 0446 hrs, all hell broke loose as the big bomber hurtled across the airfield on its belly. All eight on board escaped injury but this incident certainly changed Middleton from a rather pessimistic, lonely individual to a completely different, more out-going and happy person, perhaps because he was feeling glad to be alive.

Pathfinder opportunity

Middleton became the skipper of his own crew for the first time on the night of 31 July at the helm of Stirling Mk I, W7566 'OJ-C', as part of a large raid to Düsseldorf. It was one of 61 Stirlings that took part, and while they all returned safely, it was the Wellingtons from the OTUs which bore the brunt of the losses on this occasion.

It is not clear whether or not Middleton and his crew were selected at the time by the well-known 'poacher' of crews, Wg Cdr 'Hamish' Mahaddie, but, on 25 August, they were posted to 7 Squadron, still at Oakington and still flying the Stirling, although 7 Squadron had now become one of the founding squadrons of the fledgling 8 Group, aka the Pathfinders, along with 35, 83 and 156 Squadrons. 7 Squadron had only participated in its second Pathfinder Force (PFF) operation the night before Middleton and his crew arrived, destined to make their debut three nights later in a raid on Nuremburg. Taking off from Oakington at 2038 hrs in Stirling Mk I, R9158 'MG-E', the raid did not go well for Middleton's crew, who found themselves, through poor navigation, more than 90 miles SSE of the target, over

Munich. On his return, Middleton was forced to divert to Manston because of a lack of fuel. The four Hercules engines stopped as the bomber touched down and, with no power available for the brakes, it careered into a line of Spitfires before settling next to the station armoury, minus its wings.

Mahaddie was unimpressed and, after they arrived back at Oakington, the 7 Squadron CO gave Middleton an ultimatum; have your navigator replaced or leave the PFF. Without hesitation, he refused and, as a result, Middleton and his crew found themselves back at 149 Squadron on 2 September.

Over the coming weeks, Middleton experienced several close shaves on operations which ranged from 'gardening' sorties in the Bay of Biscay, to raids on Wilhelmshaven and Kiel and, on 23 October, the first of four trips over the Alps to Italy. It was a sortie to Turin, Middleton's 29th operation, on 28 November 1942, that would put the young Australian into RAF history books.

A final return to Turin

By now, Middleton's crew was highly experienced, including his air gunners, two of whom had already completed their 30 operation quota but had decided to remain with their pilot until his tour of duty was completed. The front air gunner, Sgt John W Mackie from Clackmannanshire, was on his 31st operation, the mid-upper air gunner, ex-gamekeeper Sgt Douglas Cameron was highly experienced, and the rear gunner, Sgt Harold Gough from Scarborough, was about to embark on his 33rd operation. Second pilot was Flt Sgt Leslie A Hyder, the navigator was FO George R Royde, wireless operator was Plt Off Norman E Skinner and the flight engineer was 19-year-old Sgt James E Jeffrey. For this operation, a return to Turin, Middleton had been allocated Stirling Mk I, BF372 'OJ-H', not the best example of the breed as it had quite a reputation for making the ground crews' lives a bit of a misery.

With an 8,000 lb bomb load and full fuel tanks, Middleton knew from the outset that this would be one of the most challenging operations of his career. At 1814 hrs, Middleton lifted BF372 off Lakenheath's long runway, setting a course SSE towards the target which was 600 miles away. Altitude was always an issue with the Stirling, thanks to that short wing, but BF372 would not even reach the average operating height of 16,500 ft, as the bomber refused to climb above 12,000 ft. At the lower height, fuel consumption was higher and, on top of that, the auto-pilot, for ever nicknamed 'George', decided that it was not taking part in that night's operation. It was already decision time for Middleton and, after a discussion with Jeffrey, they worked out that the operation could continue, but there would be very little fuel in hand for the return trip. The lack of altitude would also mean that the aircraft would need to be

A typical example of a 149 (East India) Stirling at Lakenheath in the summer of 1943. The unit re-equipped from the Wellington Mk I to the Stirling Mk I in November 1941 followed by the Mk III, which remained until September 1944.

navigated, by Royde, through the Alps rather than over them. The range averaged 15,000 ft in height.

Mountain dead ahead

Without a hint of moonlight to help them through the treacherous mountains, Middleton steered the Stirling between the peaks, which were just visible by the snow on their summits. The fuel situation had also deteriorated because of a headwind, although by then, Middleton was more concerned about not flying into a mountain than running out of fuel. Mackie, with a grandstand view from the front turret, provided Middleton with a running commentary as peaks approached and passed. Stress levels were particularly high during this stage of the operation, although the tension was relieved when Mackie calmly said to Gough in the rear turret, 'I hope I see the next mountain before you.'

'Mountain dead ahead,' shouted Mackie which suddenly focussed the crew again, and immediately Middleton was convinced the bomber had flown into a dead end. The bomb doors were opened and just as Middleton was about to give the order to jettison, Mackie shouted again, 'It's there. Look. To starboard.' So it was, Turin in its full glory, already being illuminated by the PFF ahead, although 5 Group arrived over the target first before the Pathfinders had chance to mark the target.

After a quick fuel check with Jeffrey, Middleton calmly announced, 'Right, we're going down'. Only moments after they cleared the Alps, the Italian defences opened fire, initially striking the Stirling in the port wing which not only made a large hole but also sent shrapnel pinging around the fuselage. Middleton's concentration was not disrupted as he continued his weaving decent, levelling out at 2,000 ft with the help of Hyder.

The high level of accuracy of the Italian guns continued when BF372 was hit again, this time in the cockpit between Middleton and Hyder's seats. The windscreen was shattered and shrapnel hit Hyder in both legs. Skinner, located further behind, was also wounded in the leg. An icy wind entered the cockpit through the broken windscreen while Middleton sat motionless in his seat. All the Australian could say was, 'I'm hit,' before slumping over the controls. He was seriously injured; a piece of shrapnel had hit him on the right side of his face, removing the eye and exposing the bone of his cheek and temple. With Middleton seemingly a goner, Hyder, in considerable pain, managed to pull back on the control column before the bomber entered a final dive, recovering the Stirling at just 800 ft above the ground.

As Hyder began to gain altitude, Middleton suddenly came round, helping his second pilot to climb to 1,500 ft before dropping the bomb load onto the city.

Middleton then ordered Hyder to move to the rest bunk area to get his wounds dressed while Skinner remained at his station, not mentioning a word about his own injuries. Mackie left his turret to support his pilot, standing alongside him and guiding him onto a course in an effort to get the bomber away from flak. In the meantime, Cameron left his turret to attend to Hyder who insisted on returning to the cockpit despite suffering great pain and losing a large amount of blood.

Getting his crew home

There was nothing that could be done to prevent the fierce slipstream from entering the cockpit and Middleton simply hunkered down and prepared for the journey home as he had done many times before. Several options were on the table at this point, including setting course across the Mediterranean towards North Africa to avoid the Alps, or making for neutral Switzerland, just a short distance away, where they would be interned but looked after very quickly. However, Middleton chose the most daunting option of all, the four-hour flight back to England.

Royde gave Middleton a course for home and then ordered his crew to start throwing out all non-essential pieces of equipment from the bomber which ranged from the oxygen bottles to the sextant; even the aircraft's guns were sent falling to earth. Middleton managed to guide the Stirling back through the Alps, supported by Mackie every inch of the way, while Hyder had returned to his seat, dipping in and out of consciousness as his damaged body battled the pain. What agony Middleton must have been going through is unimaginable but, against the odds, he managed to fly the bomber safely back through the Alps and continued, mile by mile, across the French countryside towards his goal.

Not long after clearing the mountains, the Stirling was coned by a number of searchlights. Instinctively, and remarkably, Middleton summoned the strength to throw the bomber into the required manoeuvres needed to shake them off without a shot being fired. Remaining silent throughout, it was obvious to Mackie that the pain was taking its toll on his pilot and the effects of shock were taking hold. As the bomber crossed the French coast, it came under fire yet again as a few coastal guns tried their luck but this was one aircraft that was not going to be finished off that easily. Finally, the English coast began to loom ahead as Middleton asked Jeffrey for the last time what the fuel situation was like. He replied, 'No more than five minutes flying, skipper,' at which point the crew prepared for a ditching in the Channel.

Middleton had other ideas though, pulling the Stirling up to 2,500 ft, he was adamant that he was going to give his crew every chance of survival. Crossing the coast at Dymchurch at just before 0300 hrs, Middleton flew towards the small village

Surrounded by fellow NCO aircrew, Ron Middleton's coffin lies 'in state' within RAF Mildenhall's small chapel.

of Newchurch and then turned south-west, parallel with the coast, before ordering his crew to bail out. Their odds of survival were dramatically improved over land rather than in the cold of the Channel.

By this point, Hyder was rapidly succumbing to his own wounds but Mackie helped the second pilot to reach the escape hatch before pushing him out, placing his hand on the 'D' ring of his ripcord. Cameron, Gough and Royde all vacated safely followed by Skinner who left his wireless station for the first and last time despite two wounds to his leg. As Skinner left the aircraft, the Stirling turned south back over the sea, moments before the wireless operator smashed through the roof of an old hut close to a cottage.

Laying down his life for his friends

The loyal Mackie and Jeffrey did manage to leave the bomber but whether they were too late or succumbed to the cold of the Channel is not clear. Both their bodies were recovered by a naval rescue launch later that day. Of Middleton and his aircraft, there was no sign. The brave Australian had saved the lives of five of his crew by sticking to his word and bringing them home.

The award of the VC for Middleton's actions that night was announced on 13 January 1943, while all of the surviving members of the group were awarded the DFC or DFM for their part. It was not until 1 February 1943 that the sea gave up the body of Ron Middleton as his remains were washed up on Shakespeare Beach, Dover. His body was transported to Mildenhall on 4 February where the coffin was laid upon a catafalque inside the airfield's small chapel. His coffin was surrounded by aircrew SNCOs all-night and, the following morning, on 5 February, Plt Off* Rawdon Hume Middleton VC, RAAF was laid to rest with full military honours in St John's church cemetery, Beck Row. (Row D, Grave 1)

*Middleton was unaware that the notification of his commission had come through at Lakenheath on 14 November, almost two weeks before his final flight, which is why his gravestone gives his rank as Plt Off R H Middleton VC.

Massacre over Chouigui

Hugh Malcolm
(4 December 1942)

Pre-war Regular

orn in Broughton Ferry, Dundee, on 2 May 1917, Hugh Gordon Malcolm joined the RAF on 9 January 1936. Passing through the RAF College at Cranwell, Malcolm gained his wings in December 1937 and that month was posted to 26 Squadron at Catterick to fly the Lysander. At the beginning of the war, Malcolm passed through several different units before being appointed as a flight commander in 18 Squadron at Wattisham, flying the Blenheim Mk IV, in April 1942. The squadron was heavily involved in night intruder operations and even Bomber Command operations. The squadron contributed to the first '1,000-bomber' raid in May and saw out its days with the Blenheim Mk IV in Bomber Command service in August. Declared non-operational, the squadron not only awaited new equipment but also a move overseas. After moving to West Raynham, the new equipment turned out to be the unpopular Blenheim Mk V but, in September, Malcolm was promoted to wing commander, becoming the squadron's new commanding officer. He was received with far more enthusiasm than the Blenheim Mk V. By October, 18 Squadron, along with 13, 114 and 614, had been chosen to support the forthcoming Operation *Torch* under 326 Wing, and they were all settled at Blida, Algeria, by early November 1942.

Daylight raid

On 17 November 1942, Wg Cdr Malcolm led his unit's Blenheim Mk Vs into action

FO (later Wg Cdr) Hugh Gordon Malcolm VC.

A line of Bristol Blenheim Mk Vs at Canrobert airfield in Algeria.

for the first time in an attack on Bizerta airfield in Tunisia. A daylight operation carried out at low level without fighter escort was no place for the Mk V and, after running into bad weather on their return, two Blenheims collided and two more were shot down by German fighters. Bizerta was attacked again eleven days later, this time more successfully, with Malcolm leading the way by making several strafing passes over the target.

On 4 December, eleven Blenheims from 326 Wing were moved to a forward airfield at Souk-el-Arba for tactical operations in support of Allied troops. At 0915 hrs, Malcolm led six Blenheim Mk Vs in search of enemy troops in the Chouigui area but instead attacked an enemy airfield ten miles north. After returning to Canrobert to refuel, all eleven Blenheims returned to Souk-el-Arba to await further orders.

These duly came one hour after landing, calling for the Blenheims to return to the same area that they had just attacked, which would mean another daylight raid without fighter escort.

Eleven Blenheim Mk Vs were readied for the operation and, at 1515 hrs, were led from Souk-el-Arba by Wg Cdr Malcolm, flying BA875 'W' of 18 Squadron, with Plt Off J Robb navigating and Plt Off J Grant DFC as wireless operator/air gunner. On take-off, one Blenheim burst the tyre of its tail wheel and slewed off the runway, while the remaining ten tucked together in close formation. Twenty minutes later, BA825 of 614 Squadron developed engine trouble and was forced to crash-land 15 miles east of Souk-el-Arba. The crew escaped uninjured. With Malcolm still firmly in the lead, he now had four Mk Vs from 13 Squadron and four from 614 Squadron close behind him. As the formation entered the battle zone, enemy observers alerted the closest Luftwaffe airfield and Gruppen I and II/Jg2 were in the air in no time to intercept the Blenheims.

Once Malcolm had reached the objective, the small force began their bombing runs but they were immediately 'bounced' by over 50 Bf109s, which quickly tore into the Blenheims. The Mk Vs stood no chance as, one by one, they were sent plunging into the desert in flames. The Luftwaffe later claimed to have shot down all nine Blenheims, although it transpired that three managed to struggle back over Allied lines where they all crash-landed. It is most likely that Malcolm's Blenheim was the last to be shot down that day, crashing in flames 15 miles west of the target. Three Allied soldiers found the wreckage of BA875 and, despite the intense heat, managed to remove the body of Plt Off Robb while Malcolm and Grant, most likely already dead, were consumed by the flames.

Wg Cdr Malcolm's courage and determination to carry out his duty, regardless of the danger, and with the odds stacked against him, led to his being posthumously awarded the VC on 27 April 1943.

The Kiwi Great Escaper

Leonard Trent
(3 May 1943)

Independent service

The RNZAF has worked side by side with the RAF since Britain donated a pair of Blériot Monoplanes to New Zealand in 1913. Known as the New Zealand Permanent Air Force from 1923, the liaison between the two air forces grew stronger in 1926, when, in an agreement drawn up at the Imperial Conference, RAF and RNZAF officers would be attached to each other's service for experience and additional training. Our next VC recipient took part in one of these exchanges with the RAF in July 1938, by which time, the NZPAF officially had become the RNZAF, an independent service, on 1 April 1937.

Leonard Henry Trent was born in Nelson, New Zealand, on 14 April 1915; the son of a dentist, it was after his family moved to Takaka that, at the tender age of seven, he experienced flight for the first time during a joyride. Hooked on flying from then on, Trent completed his education at Nelson College in 1934.

Trent decided to join the RNZAF in January 1934 and, after being accepted for pilot training, he was sent to Wigram. Following basic flying training, he qualified as a bomber pilot and, in July 1938, as part of the exchange scheme, he made the long journey to England to join 15 Squadron Abingdon which had just re-equipped with the Fairey Battle in June. As part of the Advanced Air Strike Force, 15 Squadron was called to arms the day before the Second World War broke out and the unit moved to Béthenoville on 2 September 1939. Four days later, 15 Squadron began the first of only a handful of armed reconnaissance operations before settling at Conde/Vaux on 11 September. Trent only flew one operation during this period – an armed

A young Leonard Trent flanked by Jack Edwards (left) and Roy Max on the day of their wings graduation at Wigram in 1938.

reconnaissance at 20,000 ft over the Siegfried Line during which the oxygen system failed, forcing the crew to descend and make an early return to Vaux. The squadron was back in England, at Wyton, on 10 December 1939, where they would re-equip with the Blenheim Mk IV. Once the war gained momentum, and following the swift invasion of the Low Countries and France in May 1940, 15 Squadron carried out operations from Alconbury and Wyton in a fruitless period of sorties which saw high losses as France fell in June.

Trent was posted to 17 OTU at Upwood on 1 July 1940, a tour of duty that was perceived as 'a rest' from operations although very often the chances of survival were only marginally better than running the gauntlet against the enemy. On one occasion, Trent took off in a Douglas Boston for a familiarisation flight, only for the starboard Cyclone to burst into flames as the bomber lifted off the runway. Trent calmly made a low-level circuit of the airfield before putting the bomber back down on the runway, by which time the wing was virtually engulfed in flames. For this excellent piece of flying, Trent received a Commendation and, at the same time, a DFC for his tour of duty with 15 Squadron.

Trent was promoted to squadron leader after completing his tour with 17 OTU and, on 9 March 1942, was posted to 2 Group Headquarters at Castle Hill House, Huntingdon. Never comfortable away from the cockpit, Trent was allowed to return to operational flying and on 20 August was posted to 487 (New Zealand) Squadron, under the control of 2 Group, as 'B' Flight Commander. The unit had only been formed at Feltwell five days earlier and did not receive its first Lockheed Ventura Mk II bombers until 16 September.

Ki te mutunga (Through to the end)

487 Squadron first went into action on 6 December 1942 as part of a 93-strong force in a raid against the Philips radio and valve factories in Eindhoven, under the name Operation *Oyster*. The raid was a success but casualties were high; nine Venturas, four Bostons and a Mosquito failed to return. Poor weather disrupted 2 Group operations until late January 1943 as they continued with heavily escorted daylight attacks against short-range targets, more familiarly referred to by the RAF as *Ramrods*.

487 Squadron made the short move to Methwold on 3 April 1943 and after quickly settling in, continued operations the following day with an attack on a shipyard in Rotterdam. By early May 1943, Trent had already carried out 23 operational sorties and clearly was already being thought of as an officer with a future in the RAF because he was offered a Staff College

course. Trent politely declined, preferring to remain on operations and driven by the fact that he stood a good chance of becoming the CO of 487 Squadron, a position at the time that was held by Wg Cdr G J Grindell, whose tour of duty was coming to an end.

On 2 May, twelve Venturas from 464 Squadron, accompanied by twelve Bostons,

Nicknamed 'The Pig' in RAF service, the Lockheed Ventura did not enjoy the operational success of its older sibling the Hudson. Having formed with the type in later 1942, 487 Squadron dispensed with Venturas in favour of the highly capable Mosquito B Mk VI from August 1943.

attacked the steelworks at Ijmuiden but only the Venturas hit the target. As a result, 2 Group Headquarters issued orders to attack the target again the following day using six Bostons from 107 Squadron.

Change of plan

When the crews of 487 Squadron rose for an early briefing on 3 May 1943, they were under the impression that the target for the day was Flushing docks. It was only when they were just about to board their Venturas that the operation was cancelled. Having returned to the briefing room after lunch, the crews were presented with the new power station target, on the outskirts of Amsterdam, code-named *Ramrod* 16. The unit were to provide the main diversion for 107 Squadron with twelve Venturas. Fighter escort would be provided by three groups of Spitfires and Mustangs made up from nine squadrons. The raid would be carried in two formations of six aircraft and it was the toss of a coin that decided who would be leading the squadron that day – Wg Cdr Grindell or Trent. Trent won.

Trent would be at the controls of Ventura B Mk II, AJ209 'EG-V', with navigator/bomb-aimer, Flt Lt V Phillips, wireless operator FO R D C Thomas, and mid-upper gunner, Sgt W Trenery ('Tren') as his crew. The Ventura, the military derivative of the Lodestar transport, was a latecomer into Bomber Command service and, as such, was wholly inadequate for the European theatre by 1943. Capable of carrying up to 2,500 lb of bombs, the Ventura defended itself with a pair of .303 machine guns in a dorsal turret, two more .303 in a ventral position, and the pilot had a pair of fixed forward-firing .50 and two depressible .303 machine guns.

At 1643 hrs, Trent led the first formation of six Venturas away from Methwold. Six was soon reduced to five when Sgt Barker was forced to return after his escape hatch became detached.

The Luftwaffe ready and waiting

It was not long before the first of the escorting fighters joined the Ventura formation as they all crossed the east coast together. Tucking in close to the bombers, the formation steered towards the Dutch coast just a few feet above the waves so as not to alert the enemy that they were on their way. However, they need not have bothered, because several miles ahead, the Spitfires of 122 and 453 Squadrons, who were meant to draw the enemy away from the bombers' route, decided to climb as they crossed the enemy coast, which instantly alerted all of the Luftwaffe's fighters in the area. This factor, combined with a visit by the German Governor of Holland to the town of Haarlem, a mere five miles from the bombers' course, sealed the operation's fate as additional fighters had been drawn into the area to cover his visit. Having detected 122 and 453 Squadrons the German forces were convinced that Haarlem was the target and long before Trent's formation reached the coast, let alone the target, considerably more enemy fighters were in the air than usual. At least 70 Bf109s and Fw190s were lying in wait.

As Trent's formation approached the coast, according to the brief, the Venturas climbed to the required bombing height of 12,000 ft, while the Spitfires re-positioned themselves 150 yds above and 500 yds out on each corner of the bombers. AJ209 had a VHF radio designed to pick up enemy radio messages and thus warn the crew if an interception was forthcoming. On this occasion, the tightly packed aircraft blanked out the signal to Trent's aircraft and the first warning he received was from his own wireless operator who was peering out of the bomber's astrodrome. His early comment was a classic piece of military understatement, 'Here's a whole shower of fighters coming down out of the sun – they may be Spitfires. Hell's teeth, they're 190s and 109's! Watch 'em, Tren.'

With the target just ten minutes away, the Venturas tightened up while the Fw190s clinically attacked the Spitfires, forcing them away from the bomber formation which was now exposed to at least 30 Bf109s. Attacked from the stern and the beam, the first victim was Flt Lt A V Duffill in AE916 which was riddled from nose to tail with cannon fire and, with both engines ablaze, dropped away from the formation with two wounded crew aboard. Incredibly, Duffill managed to nurse AE916 all the way back to Methwold while two who had turned to follow were quickly despatched by the enemy.

Approaching Haarlem, another three Venturas were shot down while Trent continued to manoeuvre out of the line of fire. As Trent began his final run into the target, two more Venturas were sent earthbound, leaving just three. One Bf109 came in hard and fast but made the fatal error of turning in front of Trent's aircraft which unhesitatingly opened fire with all four machine guns. At a range of just 100yds, the Bf109 stood no chance and its wings rocked before falling away to the ground. At that point, another Ventura dropped away from the ever-decreasing formation, its port engine pouring flame and smoke.

As the last two Venturas closed on the power station, Trent focussed on his instruments while he received instructions from Phillips, who was now in the bomb aimer's position in the nose of the aircraft. As Phillips shouted 'bombs gone', Trent lifted his head to find that he was the last Ventura in the air. He then made the split-second decision to dive down low to give his aircraft and crew some chance of survival. However, just as Trent was about to push the column forward, an explosion rocked the aircraft, leaving the controls lifeless in his hands. With all the cables cut to the flying surfaces, it was clearly time to leave and Trent ordered his crew to bail out. Still waggling the column and the rudder pedals in the vain hope that some control could be restored, Trent watched as Phillips headed towards the rear fuselage. Moments later, the Ventura decided enough was enough, reared up, stalled and then slowly slumped onto its back before beginning a dramatic inverted high speed spin. Trent managed to open his escape hatch but the colossal centrifugal forces created by such a situation kept him firmly in his seat.

At this point, Trent, understandably, would have thought his days were numbered until, suddenly, the bomber exploded into an unrecognisable collection of jagged metal components falling to earth. Remarkably, in amongst the debris, Trent found himself at 7,000 ft following the remnants of his Ventura towards the ground. With his hand firmly clasping the 'D' ring of his ripcord, he did not pull his chute until he was at 3,000 ft. Not long after, he landed in a ploughed field on the edge of Amsterdam, while the bulk of his aircraft with Thomas and Trenery still inside, crashed into the Kometen Polder. Minutes later, German soldiers captured Trent, who was about to be driven away when Phillips joined him in the same vehicle. Both would begin a lengthy period as POWs.

'The Great Escape'

Being a relatively senior officer, Trent was put through the mill for a few weeks by German interrogators, including a fortnight of solitary confinement. Having survived this trauma without given away much more than his name, rank and number, Trent was sent to the officers' POW camp at Stalag Luft III located near the then German town of Sagan. Not content to serve out his time for good behaviour, Trent joined the now famous escape committee under the stoic leadership of Roger Bushell. Trent soon found himself involved in what would become one of the most daring and well organised mass escapes of the Second World War.

When the escape took place on the night of 24 March 1944, Trent was one of the last to leave the tunnel at 0500 hrs. However, as he emerged and, only seconds from making his dash to the tree line, a German patrol appeared, forcing Trent to lie motionless in the snow for a few agonising moments. One soldier literally stepped over him, at which point another would-be escaper was spotted by the patrol bringing the whole exercise to a swift conclusion. Within no time, Trent was back behind the wire while 76 others were making their bid for freedom. Trent's re-capture would be a blessing in disguise because, out of the 76, only three managed to escape while 50 of those caught were mercilessly shot as an example to other POWs on the orders of Adolf Hitler.

Trent returned to England in May 1945 and it was only then that the full story of the Ventura raid came to light. As a result, on 1 March 1946 Trent was awarded the

Wing Commander L H Trent DFC VC during his tour as the CO of 214 Squadron from March 1956. The unit took part in the Suez crisis and, on 1 September 1956, Trent flew a Valiant non-stop from Lowring AFB, Maine, direct to RAF Marham, the first non-stop Atlantic flight by a V-bomber.

VC for his leadership and devotion to duty. He would serve in the post-war RAF, beginning with the role of Chief Flying Instructor at Oakington in the early 1950s followed by a tour as the new CO of the re-formed 214 (Federated Malay States) Squadron at Marham in March 1956, by then equipped with the Vickers Valiant. Promoted to group captain, he became the station commander of Wittering from 1 July 1959 and, in 1962, served as ADC to the Queen. After a period attached to the British Defence Staff and later the British Embassy in the USA, Trent retired from the RAF in April 1965, after 27 years' service, and moved to Western Australia with his wife, Ursula, and their three children. In 1977, the family moved to Matheson Bay, Auckland and on 19 May 1986 Gp Capt Leonard Henry Trent DFC, VC, passed away in North Shore Hospital, Takapuna at the age of 71.

The Dam Busters

Guy Gibson
(16/17 May 1943)

'Very determined character'

An individual who has had much written about him over the past few years, was a household name during the Second World War and remains so to this day. Guy Penrose Gibson was born on 12 August 1918 to Alexander James and Leonora Mary Gibson in Simla, India. At that time his father was working for the Imperial Indian Forestry Service and was later promoted to Chief Conservator of Forests in the Simla Hill States region. When Gibson was aged six, his parents separated and, as would be the tradition at that time, his mother gained custody of Guy, his older brother Alexander and his sister Joan.

Leonora, more familiarly known as 'Nora', decided to return with her three children to England. They initially settled in her native Cornwall at Penzance and Gibson's education began at the West Cornwall College. Once his mother had moved again to London, he had a spell as a border at Earl's Avenue and St George's School, Folkestone. Gibson then settled at St Edward's School, Oxford from 1932 which was also attended by a character by the name of Douglas Bader a few years earlier. Gibson was never strong academically but, as with virtually all future RAF officers he was an all-rounder at sports, playing for the Rugby Second XV. Described by his housemaster as a 'very determined character', Gibson showed that he would achieve, regardless of his lack of ability in the world of academia.

Determined to fly

Gibson set his sights very high from the outset with regard to a future career as a pilot, not just any old pilot, but a civilian test pilot. He applied for such a position at Vickers and, after receiving a personal letter from chief test pilot Captain Joseph 'Mutt' Summers, who advised him to learn to fly by joining the RAF, Gibson did just that. He was initially rejected by the RAF's Medical Board because he was too short in the leg, but after a second attempt, which he passed, he was accepted for a short service commission in late 1936.

Gibson's RAF flying career began on 16 November 1936, when he began his ab initio training with the Bristol Flying School at Yatesbury, followed by 'square bashing' at Uxbridge in January 1937. Commissioned on 31 January 1937 as an Acting Pilot Officer, Gibson was posted to 6 FTS at Netheravon, which included a spell with No.3 ATS at RAF Sutton Bridge. Gibson passed out of his flying training on 31 August 1937 with an 'average' rating for both his ground exams and his flying ability. Bearing in mind that Gibson's whole aim at the time was to gain experience before becoming a civilian test pilot, the young airman was declared as 'below average' when it came to his condescending attitude towards all non-commissioned servicemen.

Civilian career on hold – permanently

Gibson's first posting was in September 1937, to 83 Squadron at Turnhouse which had only reformed the previous month with the Hawker Hind light bomber. Gibson quickly settled into the superior (in his eyes) lifestyle of a commissioned officer with a public school background. This air of arrogance soon gained the young Gibson the nickname of the 'Bumptious Bastard' from his ground crew.

The squadron moved to Scampton, under 5 Group control on 14 March 1938, and it was here that the unit converted to the twin-engine Hampden, which at the time, was the perfect multi-engine machine for those seeking a civilian career to gain experience. After taking a navigation course at Hamble in April 1939, Gibson once again finished with an 'average' rating, although the instructor did record the profound comment, 'could do well'. On the verge of leaving the RAF, Gibson was retained because of the Abyssinian situation and in June 1939 he was promoted to Flying Officer.

Gibson's first operation of the Second World War was the day it started, 3 September 1939, when he was one of a handful of pilots, led by Squadron Leader L S Snaith AFC, to attack the German fleet near Wilhelmshaven. No ships were found owing to bad weather. Gibson was destined not to fly another operation until

11 April 1940, but the following five-month period would be the most intensive of his career with 34 sorties flown. He was awarded the DFC on 9 July 1940 and despite flying a bomber, was credited with a 'probable kill' when he attacked a Dornier Do215 on return from a raid on Lorient on 27 August.

Promoted to Flight Lieutenant on 3 September 1940, Gibson was withdrawn from operations for a rest three days after a raid on Berlin on 23 September. The 'rest' was a posting to 14 OTU, Cottesmore, as a flying instructor but he was soon posted to 16 OTU at Upper Heyford where he itched for a return to operational flying.

Night fighter pilot

During his time with 83 Squadron, the AOC of 5 Group was Air Marshal Sir Arthur Harris, who had singled Gibson out as one of the most spirited pilots within his command. When the senior staff of Fighter Command began a trawl for would-be night fighter pilots from Bomber Command, Gibson was one of a small band of willing volunteers. As a result Flight Lieutenant Gibson was posted to 29 Squadron on 13 November, under the command of Sqn Ldr C Widdows stationed at Digby and Wellingore. Widdows was working hard to re-build the unit, which had been suffering from poor morale, due in part to the fact that the squadron was equipped with the unsuitable Blenheim Mk IF night fighter. One of the many changes was to bring Gibson in as 'A' Flight commander; an unpopular move with many of the long-serving members of the unit who thought they should have been promoted to the role.

Gibson flew six unsuccessful sorties in the Blenheim, before the squadron re-equipped with the much-improved Beaufighter Mk IF, and under Widdows' close supervision the morale and success of the unit were quickly turned around. Gibson began his conversion to the AI-equipped Beaufighter on 1 December, followed by his first operational sortie with a Beaufighter just nine days later. Success came for Gibson and his AI operator Sergeant R H James on 12 March 1941, but it could not be confirmed, while two days later a Heinkel He111 was brought down near Skegness. On the night of 8 April the tables were turned when a Ju88 stalked Gibson's Beaufighter back to Wellingore and attacked just as he was landing. Gibson was uninjured but his AI operator Sgt Bell was wounded in the leg. With James as his observer again, an enemy bomber was attacked on 23 April, while four days later, the squadron's potential hunting ground was improved with a move to West Malling.

Promoted to Acting Squadron Leader on 29 June, Gibson's claims began to mount, including a He111 of 8/KG4 which was blown apart over Sheerness on 6

July. Claims continued up to 21 October, when a pair of Ju87s were attacked off Dover and by the time Gibson's tour came to an end he could claim three aircraft destroyed, one probable and four damaged, all with Sgt James as his observer, who was awarded the DFM for his efforts. Gibson had flown 99 Beaufighter operations and was awarded a bar to his DFC on 10 September, but by then, had already grown tired of night fighters and craved a return to bomber operations.

Posted to 51 OTU at Cranfield as chief flying instructor, following his final Beaufighter sortie on 15 December, Gibson immediately began trying to return to bomber operations. Sir Arthur Harris, who became AOC of Bomber Command in February 1942, had promised in 1940 to help Gibson as much as he could and following an interview, he decided to promote him to Wing Commander and put him in charge of a Lancaster squadron. Harris had suggested 207 Squadron, while the AOC 5 Group, Air-Vice Marshal Slessor recommended 106 Squadron, where Gibson duly arrived on 13 April 1942.

Back to Bomber Ops

Now on his third operational tour, Gibson took command of 106 Squadron at Coningsby during the twilight weeks of the unit's association with the Vulture-powered Manchester. Despite the bomber's failings, morale was not as low as expected, being bolstered by Gibson's leadership. The young Wing Commander flew his first Manchester operation on 22 April and during early May the first Lancasters began to arrive.

During Gibson's eleven-month tenure as Commanding Officer of 106 Squadron, he led from the front at all times and his relentless aggression towards every target filtered through to his crews. He was still a man who preferred the company of officers, and his treatment of NCOs left a lot to be desired. He did not make his first operational flight in a Lancaster until 8/9 July, with FO Dave Shannon (who would later take part in Operation *Chastise*), on a trip to Wilhelmshaven.

In August 1942 the squadron was tasked with trialling two different types of bomb sight which were designed to work in conjunction with the 5,294 lb Capital Ship Bomb (CSB). It was specifically 'C' Flight of 106 Squadron who was tasked with testing the weapon, which was tested operational at Gdynia on 27/28 August 1942, where it was thought the *Gneisenau* and *Scharnhorst* were anchored. The Germans' only aircraft carrier, the *Graf Zeppelin* was also located at Gdynia and it was hoped the new CSB would sink at least one of these significant warships. Nine Lancasters took part in the raid, although only three were loaded with CSBs. In the end, the harbour was covered in haze and the three weapons were dropped on the dock area instead. Neither the weapon nor the raid was a success, through no fault of the squadron, but the preparations that Gibson put 'C' Flight through were noted by Harris and the AOC 5 Group, Air-Vice Marshal Coryton.

Gibson continued to lead from the front in raids on Germany, Italy and France, the last including the famous low-level daylight raid to Le Creusot on 17 October 1942. He was awarded the DSO on 6 November 1942 followed by a Bar to his DSO in early 1943. Gibson flew his final 106 Squadron operation on 15 March 1943, to Stuttgart and, on his return, prepared himself for a spell of leave in Cornwall.

617 Squadron formed

On 18 March, Gibson was ordered to attend an interview at HQ 5 Group at St Vincents, Grantham, where he was asked by Air-Vice Marshal Cochrane if he was prepared to take on one more operation. During a further interview the following day he was told that he would command a brand new squadron, while all the detail he was given at this stage, was that it would require a great deal of low flying at night and the target had to be attacked before 19 May. Against traditional policy, Gibson, with the help of Grp Capt Satterly, was allowed to choose his own aircrew which would include a large number of individuals who had either flown with him, or served with him. Only the wireless operator, Flt Lt R E G Hutchinson, volunteered from Gibson's 106 Squadron.

On 23 March 1943, 617 Squadron was officially formed at Scampton, although Gibson had already begun to make himself at home on the first floor of No.2 Hangar two days earlier. On 24 March, Gibson met Barnes Wallis for the first time at his home in Burhill, not far from Weybridge, and although the Vickers designer could not reveal the targets, he could reveal the type of weapon that was to be used. Code-named 'Upkeep', the 9,250 lb cylindrical mine became known as the 'bouncing bomb'. To carry the weapon, the Lancaster was modified into the B Mk III (Special), which included removal of the bomb doors with the exposed ends faired off, a pair of v-shaped struts to hold the mine, and a hydraulic motor and drive belt which could spin the mine at 500 rpm.

From 28 March, the first of many low-level exercises began, combined with ever-longer cross-country flights and within a month, Gibson was happy to report that his new unit could fly accurately at low-level at night and to a height of just 60 ft over water. Before the end of March the targets were revealed to Gibson as the Möhne, Eder and Sorpe dams located in North Rhine-Westphalia. As a result, training was adjusted to include a variety of reservoirs with dams, spread across the country. The first full-blown rehearsal was flown by 617 Squadron on 10 May, even though the first successful release of a live Upkeep mine was not actually achieved until the following day. Between 11 and 14 May, the majority of the crews were able to carry out a practice drop at Reculver, including Gibson in Lancaster B Mk III, ED932, 'AJ-G', the same aircraft that he would use for the operation.

Operation *Chastise*

The first of three briefings took place at 1200 hrs on 16 May 1943 which was specifically for the benefit of the pilots and navigators, followed by a bomb aimer and air gunner briefing at 1430 hrs and finally, all aircrew attended the main and final briefing at 1800 hrs, which was also attended by Barnes Wallis and Air Vice Marshal Cochrane.

19 Lancasters in three formations were detailed for the operation, code-named *Chastise*. Nine Lancasters led by Gibson were divided into three flights. Their primary target was the Möhne, then if any weapons remained after a breach occurred their secondary target was the Eder. A second formation of five Lancasters were allocated to the Sorpe, while a further five bombers would operate as an airborne 'reserve', taking off two hours after the rest and to be called upon, where necessary, to attack one of the three main targets or one of three secondary targets; the Lister, Ennepe or Diemel dams.

In company with Flt Lts J V Hopgood and H B Martin, Gibson took off at 2139 hrs and within a few minutes was crossing the Lincolnshire coast at Skegness with the other two flights not far behind. The Dutch coast was crossed at tree top level, although further south than planned, as the wind was stronger than the earlier meteorological briefing had predicted, making navigation very challenging. Despite re-adjusting the route, Gibson's flight continued to travel further south than necessary but was generally unopposed, with the exception of some light flak along the Rhine. Despite the earlier problems with navigation, the Möhne Dam was reached and, as had been described in one of the briefings, the defences were light with only one light flak battery.

Gibson carried out a single dummy run over the target, at which point, the second wave arrived, led by Sqn Ldr H M Young, accompanied by Flt Lts D J H Maltby and D J Shannon. Gibson, as expected, was the first to make a live bombing run but the mine was released too early and rather than sinking against the wall of the dam, it exploded short. It took five minutes for the water to settle before Gibson called Hopgood in to make his run, by which time the single flak battery had already gauged the position of the next attacking aircraft. Hopgood's aircraft was struck by flak, but the crew still managed to release their mine which skimmed across the water over the top of the dam and exploded on the far side destroying an electrical station. Hopgood's Lancaster was pouring flame as it flew over the dam and crashed on the far side. Again waiting for the water to return to its flat calm state,

The Möhne Dam emptying its contents into the Möhne and Ruhr rivers. While the raid was deemed a success at first, the lack of follow-up raids saw the dams quickly repaired.

Gibson called in Martin, but this time flew alongside in an effort to draw off the flak. It worked, but Martin's mine did not skim across the water cleanly, veering to one side and exploding without causing any damage. It was now Young's turn, this time accompanied by Martin, while Gibson flew in a different direction to successfully draw the flak unit away from the main attacking aircraft. It was Young's mine that was delivered the most accurately and, unbeknown to the crews, had actually caused a small breach deep in the bowels of the dam. Maltby then began his run, dropped his mine accurately and after a huge column of water was forced up by the blast, the wall of the Möhne dam let go, sending a deluge of about 330 million tons of water into the valley beyond. The code-word 'Nigger' (after Gibson's late dog and squadron mascot) was transmitted by Gibson's wireless operator, Flt Lt R E G Hutchinson, at 0056 hrs, telling HQ 5 Group that the Möhne had been breached.

All attention was then turned to the Eder. While Martin and Maltby headed for home, the third flight of the first wave arrived, comprising just Sqn Ldr H E Maudslay and Plt Off L G Knight as Flt Lt W Astell had struck power lines en route and crashed. Less than 15 minutes later the small group of Lancasters had arrived over the Eder, although Shannon found himself over the Rhebuch dam further west and was guided back to the Eder via Very lights fired from Gibson's aircraft. Defences at the Eder only consisted of a couple of sentries, but this dam was much more difficult to approach than the Möhne. Shannon was called in first, to carry out three dummy runs, followed by Maudslay who carried out two. By then, fully familiar with his intended route, Shannon started his attack. He dropped the mine accurately and it exploded but did not cause a breach. Maudslay followed, but his mine did not enter the water well, skimmed high into a parapet and exploded, the blast consuming the Lancaster which somehow managed to fly away from the target. Gibson then called up Astell to begin his attack, unaware that his bomber had crashed sometime earlier. It was then Knight's turn, who after making just one dummy run, released his mine which exploded and breached the Eder at 0154 hrs. Hutchinson then sent the code-word 'Dinghy' (Young's nickname) to HQ 5 Group indicating that the Eder had also been breached.

The second wave of Lancasters, which had been allocated the Sorpe Dam, had not faired too well on the outbound flight. Flt Lt R N G Barlow and Plt Off V W Byers had crashed en route while Flt Lt J L Munro had to turn back after being damaged by flak. Plt Off G Rice lost his mine after flying too low over the sea. Only Flt Lt K C McCarthy managed to release his mine successfully against the Sorpe, but failed to breach it.

Of the third and final wave, Plt Off L J Burpee crashed en route, while Flt Sgt K W Brown was the second and final aircraft to attack the Sorpe, but despite a successful release of the mine, failed to breach the dam. Flt Sgt W C Townsend's was the only aircraft to attack the Ennepe, and his single mine was not enough to cause a breach. Flt Sgt C T Anderson failed to reach the Sorpe because of navigation problems and running into poor weather. He returned to Scampton with his mine still on board.

The aftermath

Of the 19 Lancasters despatched from Scampton that night, eight failed to return. Of the 56 men missing, only three survived to become POWs. The attack on the Möhne was a spectacular success, the resulting release of water created by a breach 250 ft wide and nearly 300 ft deep caused a 32-ft-high tidal wave, which was still 18 ft high after reaching Schwerte, 24 miles away. Up to 1,600 people were

His Majesty King George VI with the Station Commander, Group Captain J N H Whitworth and Wing Commander G P Gibson. Modifications to the Lancasters which took part in Operation Chastise *are visible in the background.* RAF Scampton Museum

drowned, a large number of them were POWs and forced labourers. 6,500 cattle were drowned and 125 factories and 46 bridges were either destroyed or damaged, and nearly 1,000 houses were destroyed and roads and railway lines were washed away.

Of the eight surviving crews, 33 were awarded gallantry medals while their leader, Wg Cdr Guy Gibson was awarded the VC which was gazetted on 28 May 1943. A memorable mass investiture was performed by Queen Elizabeth (later Queen Mother) at Buckingham Palace on 22 June 1943.

617 Squadron was stood down after Operation *Chastise* but Gibson managed to fly another operation on 2 August before he joined Winston Churchill and a senior entourage, on a visit to Canada and the USA. While in the USA, Gibson was awarded the American Legion of Merit from General H H 'Hap' Arnold.

Gibson was back in Britain in December 1943, declared 'non-operational' and given a desk job at the Air Ministry in the Directorate of the Prevention of Accidents. Following a posting to Uxbridge in March 1944, and a course at the Staff College, Bulstrode Park, he became 'semi-operational' after a move to HQ 55 Base at East Kirkby on 12 June. He still managed to squeeze another operation in on 19 July at the controls of a 630 Squadron Lancaster before being posted again to HQ 54 Base at Coningsby. The opportunity to leave the RAF and become an MP was declined by Gibson, who, despite still being classed as 'semi-operational' continued to chase every opportunity to fly on operations. He flew three more operations from Coningsby; two as an observer in a Lockheed Lightning during August and one in a Mosquito in early September.

Gibson's thirst for operational flying saw him approach Sir Arthur Harris, who reluctantly allowed him to fly one more operational sortie, although it had to be a 'soft target'. He was detailed as Master Bomber for a 220-strong Lancaster force accompanied by ten Mosquitoes against a pair of industrial targets at Rheydt and Mönchengladbach on the evening of 19 September. Gibson would fly Mosquito B Mk XX, KB267 'E' of 627 Squadron, with Sqn Ldr J B Warwick as his navigator, who was screened from operations and was serving as the Station Navigation Officer at the time. The raid did not go well from the start, marking was poor to the extent that Gibson tried to mark the target himself. The raid was all over by 2158 hrs and without witnesses it was presumed that Gibson made his own way from the target area. Just over 30 minutes later eye witnesses saw an aircraft flying low and slow, streaming flame, close to the Dutch village of Steenbergen. One eye witness described the aircraft as 'an arc of flames curving to earth'.

Both men were given a proper funeral thanks to the persistence of the local deputy mayor, Mr Herbers and were buried in Steenbergen Roman Catholic Cemetery in a single coffin. Initially, only Warwick's full identity could be confirmed

Wing Commander Guy Gibson with four of his crew which took part in Operation Chastise on 16/17 May 1943 pictured at Scampton in July 1943. (Left to right), Gibson (pilot); Pilot Officer P M Spafford (bomb aimer); Flight Lieutenant R E G Hutchinson (wireless operator); Pilot Officer G A Deering (front air gunner) and Flying Officer H T Taerum (navigator). Not present are Sergeant J Pulford (flight engineer) and Flight Lieutenant R D Trevor-Roper (rear air gunner).

and as such, a single white cross with Warwick's full name and 'Guy Gibson' (found on a laundry tag in a sock) underneath was placed on the grave. Once the full identity of one of Britain's most decorated servicemen was revealed, a second cross was placed at the grave. Immediately after the war these were replaced by a pair of CWGC headstones.

Target Turin

Arthur Aaron
(12/13 August 1943)

From the Flying Circus to the RAF

Arthur Louis Aaron was born on 5 March 1922 in Leeds. His father, Benjamin, was a Russian Jewish immigrant and his mother hailed from Switzerland. His interest in aviation germinated at a very young age when he, like many others, first experienced flying at one of Alan Cobham's Flying Circuses.

Aaron's main education was at Roundhay Secondary School, where he won an art scholarship in 1939 and went on to Leeds College of Architecture. His enthusiasm for flying never waned and to gain more experience he joined the local Air Defence Cadet Corps (Air Training Corps from 1941). This was the springboard for a future in the RAF and, on 15 September 1941, the 19-year-old Aaron enlisted. Selected to be a pilot, Aaron was sent to the USA to begin his flying training at No.1 (British) FTS, stationed at Terrel in Texas.

Aaron passed out as a sergeant pilot on 19 June 1942 and, after returning to England, continued his flying training with 6 (P)AFU at Little Rissington. A spell with 26 OTU at RAF Wing, on Wellingtons followed, before Aaron was introduced to his future operational aircraft, the Short Stirling, at 1657 HCU at Stradishall. It was from here on 17 April 1943 that Aaron was posted to his first operational unit, 218 (Gold Coast) Squadron, stationed at Downham Market.

Piling on the sorties

As with all new crews, Aaron's was gently broken in to operations with a few 'gardening' trips; their first was over the Bay of Biscay. Promoted to flight sergeant on 1 May, Aaron was described as a good-mannered unassuming character on the ground but, once he was in the skipper's seat of a Stirling, he commanded respect and discipline from his crew who he quickly turned into a tight-knit team able to carry out a certain part of each other's tasks so that, in the event of an emergency, all would be calm and controlled rather than confused and chaotic. For example, the whole crew would have a good understanding of how to fly the aircraft, which would prove invaluable in the near future.

By early August, Aaron's experienced crew had completed 19 operations, attacking targets in France and Germany. One of those operations revealed the mettle of young Aaron when his Stirling Mk I, BK761, was hit badly by flak during the bomb run at night over Remscheid on 30/31 July. With only limited control of the aircraft, Aaron pressed on, bombed the target, and returned the Stirling to Downham Market. For this display of very cool airmanship, Aaron was awarded the DFM.

First and last trip to Italy

It was on the afternoon of 12 August 1943 that the crews of 218 Squadron gathered in the smoky briefing room which was charged with tension until the target was revealed. There was an audible sigh of relief as the large map on the wall showed the target to be Turin; a much better option than one deep in Germany such as the Ruhr, or Berlin. Aaron and his crew had not carried out a raid on Italy before and their relief was mixed with excitement, as this would be a new adventure.

For this trip, Aaron would be flying Stirling Mk I, EF452 'HA-O' with his regular crew, comprising flight engineer Sgt M M Mitchem, navigator Sgt A C Brennan RCAF, bomb aimer Flt Sgt A W Larden RCAF, wireless operator Sgt T Guy, mid-upper gunner Sgt J Richmond and rear gunner Sgt T M McCabe.

Two major raids to Italy were planned for that evening; the other involved 504 aircraft (Lancasters and Halifaxes) which would attack Milan. The Turin raid, with 152 aircraft taking part from 3 and 8 Groups, was made up of 112 Stirlings, 34 Halifaxes and six Lancasters.

Aaron lifted his heavily laden Stirling from Downham Market's main runway at 2135 hrs, just as the sun was about to dip below the horizon. While his well-oiled crew kept themselves occupied, Aaron concentrated on slowly gaining height. He had reached only 10,000 ft as the bomber stream crossed the French coast near Caen. By then, the evening had transformed into a beautiful moonlit night and, once the Stirling had clambered to 14,000 ft, Aaron decided enough was enough and levelled the aircraft out.

It was not long before the snow-covered peaks of the Alps appeared ahead, a beautiful sight, but to Aaron it was almost magical as one of his passions before joining up was rock-climbing. Gazing in wonderment at Mont Blanc, the crew's

218 (Gold Coast) Squadron was re-formed as a bomber unit at Upper Heyford in March 1936 with the Hawker Hart. The impressive Stirling joined the squadron in January 1942 at Marham but the unit later moved down the road to Downham Market. It was from this Norfolk airfield that Arthur Aaron VC carried out his final operation.

With veteran Stirling Mk I, N3721, which was flown by Aaron to Bochum on 13/14 May, providing the backdrop, two of his crew, Sgt J Richmond (right kneeling) and Sgt T M McCabe (second right kneeling) make up this 218 Squadron group.

minds were focussed back on the task ahead as the lights of Turin, which very rarely seemed to adhere to any kind of blackout precautions, appeared ahead.

Friendly fire

They approached the target and all seemed well as Aaron ordered the bomb doors to be opened. Simultaneously, Larden made himself comfortable in the bomb aimer's position. Moments later, Richmond, who had the best view of all from his mid-upper turret, voiced his concern to his pilot as another bomber crept uncomfortably close; 'Watch that bloke up front, Art.' 'Ok Rich,' replied Aaron who had leaned over to see another Stirling to starboard and slightly below of EF452. Then, within a heartbeat, all hell broke loose, combined with Richmond shouting, 'Christ, he's firing at us!' 'Fire back at him, Richie' came Aaron's swift reply, but Richmond could not bring his guns to bear on the culprit, who was shielded by EF452's wing.

Unbelievably, the rear gunner of the other Stirling had let loose with all four .303

machine guns from a range of just 250 yds. EF452 was hit from the nose to the starboard wing and back again before the lethal hail ceased. Within the navigator's compartment, Sgt Brennan fell stone dead as a single round passed through his heart, while Larden, in the nose, stared in disbelief at the neat line of holes in the side of the aircraft. The rounds missed his head by only a few inches.

Larden quickly came to his senses on hearing the voice of Mitchem who was attending to Aaron, 'My god, fellows, look at Art. Oh poor Art. Give me a hand Allan.' As Larden climbed back up into the cockpit, he was faced with a scene of utter devastation. Aaron was slumped over onto his left side, the side of his face was covered in blood from a horrific, gaping wound, while his right arm hung lifeless, barely attached to the young Yorkshireman's shattered body.

The cockpit itself had fared no better than its pilot, the instrument panel was virtually wrecked and the forward section of the windscreen had gone. Mitchem leapt into the co-pilot's seat as the Stirling, still under full power, began to dive towards the ground. Handling the throttles was proving difficult as at least two of the levers had been damaged during the attack. Larden and Mitchem, (without thinking, as they had practised many times, thanks to Aaron) changed places and, at 4,000 ft, the Canadian bomb aimer brought the aircraft under control. Mitchem and two other members of the crew then administered morphine to their pilot before moving him to the middle of the Stirling between the aircraft's main spars. However, Aaron, who had come round, was determined to know what Larden intended on doing next. While conscious, Aaron was unable to talk because of his facial injury and before he would allow his crew to carry out further medical treatment, he insisted on writing a message to Larden on the back of his deceased navigator's log telling him to head for England.

South is the only way out

At just 4,000 ft in the Alps, still with a full bomb load and one engine on the verge of overheating, Larden's predicament was not just a case of steering towards England. He had no choice but to continue south at this point, aggravated by the fact that 'George' the autopilot had also been knocked out, the trim tab cables had been severed and the hydraulic lines, which powered the rear turret, were emptying their contents into the rear fuselage. Larden let Aaron know that he had received his order, although a flight all the way home to England was rapidly becoming the least appealing option. At first, Larden steered the bomber east towards Austria but, once clear of the lower peaks of the southern Alps, he changed course in a more westerly direction with the hope of reaching Sicily.

The bomber eventually crossed the Italian coast at Spezia, at which point Larden dumped the bomb load into the sea and, after yet another check of the engines and fuel, was relieved at the controls by Mitchem. The mid-upper gunner, Richmond, also took his turn at the controls of the Stirling, while Larden and Mitchem considered their options once they arrived over Sicily. While all this had been going on, Guy had worked hard to make contact on his wireless so that they could gain a fix, as they only had a very rough idea of where they actually were. He did manage to receive a weak response and then sent a distress call to Bone in North Africa, who promptly responded. The decision had now been made for them, because Bone insisted that they should not land in Sicily but head across the Mediterranean instead.

In the midst of all that had gone before, neither Larden nor Mitchem had actually taken any time for themselves and it was only while Richmond was at the controls that they realised how lucky they had been in the hail of bullets. Larden had actually been hit twice in the right buttock and Mitchem, looking down at his shredded flying boot, had been hit by three bullets, two of them tearing the skin down to the bone.

Once relieved by Larden, Richmond returned to his skipper who had come round again enough to scrape another message, 'How navigate?' With Guy and Richmond in attendance, Aaron was re-assured that they were on course for Bone, and that all was well.

Desert sanctuary

It was another four hours before a pair of searchlight beams indicated that the African coast had been reached, but Larden, who had spotted them first, was not sure if it was actually Bone airfield. When the two beams were joined by a third, Larden made straight for them and, after being given a reciprocal heading by Guy, he headed out to sea and turned back over the airfield which had, by then, been lit.

As Larden entered the circuit a message was received that a Wellington lay wrecked at the end of the main runway. By this stage, Larden had decided to belly-land the bomber next to the main runway but, to his rear, his skipper had been woken by a combination of the aircraft's uncomfortable manoeuvres and the morphine wearing off. Incredibly, and despite his injuries, Aaron was determined to return to the cockpit and, after Mitchem made way, the two air gunners, Richmond and McCabe, helped their brave pilot back into his rightful place. Mitchem returned to his engineer's panel, while Larden remained in the co-pilot's seat. Only able to use his left arm, Aaron indicated his instructions to Larden by nodding his head towards the throttles as and when he needed more or less power. Aaron had no idea about the Wellington at the end of runway, despite Larden's warnings, and instinctively he lined the big bomber up for a standard landing approach. However, the approach did not feel right and with a nod of the head, Larden opened the throttles and Aaron guided EF452 around for a second circuit.

On Aaron's second attempt to land, he was again not happy and Larden opened the throttles for yet another circuit, much to the chagrin of Mitchem, who shouted that they had to land on the next attempt or they would run out of fuel. At 500 ft above the ground on Aaron's third attempt, he indicated that he wanted to go around again but this time Larden could not obey his skipper's orders, they had to land. Aaron attempted to open the throttles himself but Larden was having none of it and, in an act which may have haunted him for the rest of his life, he thumped his skipper across the chest, forcing him to release the controls before he collapsed into his seat.

EF452 was now on the brink of stalling, the big bomber vibrating and straining, but Larden managed to push the control column forward just in time. The Stirling pitched alarmingly towards the desert on the edge of the airfield before Larden pulled back hard on the controls. Once level, the bomber was already skimming the sand, the throttles were chopped and the Stirling briefly slid along on its belly carving a shallow trench of sand and dirt until it came to a halt; they had been in the air for over eight and half hours.

Aaron's limp body was lifted from the bomber and, within minutes, he was on an operating table in Bone's hospital. Surgeons placed priority on removing at least two bullets from the right side of Aaron's chest and, once this operation was complete, he was placed on a ward to see how well he would respond before the rest of his injuries were attended to. The rest of the crew had escaped relatively unharmed; Larden and Mitchem had their wounds attended to quickly.

'An example of courage'

While his crew waited anxiously for news of their severely injured skipper, they discovered that one bomb had 'hung-up' and they were extremely lucky that the forced-landing had not detonated the device. Larden was also presented with an alarming souvenir when one of the salvage crew gave him back his parachute harness which had been struck by two bullets, damaging the mechanism so that it was permanently in the 'release' position. This would have meant that if he had bailed out, as soon as he pulled the ripcord, he would have slipped straight through the damaged harness to his death.

The surgeons who worked on Aaron's shattered body were initially pleased with how the young airman was responding, but the news that his crew had all been dreading came through at 1500 hrs. Flt Sgt Arthur Louis Aaron DFM was buried with full military honours in Bone War Cemetery, Annaba, Algeria. It would be a few

Aaron's grave at Bone War Cemetery, Annaba, Algeria. Commonwealth War Graves Commission

weeks before his crew could relay the events that took place over Turin that night. Aaron was awarded the VC, which was published in The London Gazette on 3 November 1943. Larden was awarded the CGM, while Mitchem and Guy received the DFM.

Aaron's proud parents received their son's VC during an investiture at Buckingham Palace on 25 February 1944. In December 1953, his father Benjamin presented Aaron's medals for permanent display in the Leeds City Museum where they remain to this day. Memorials for Aaron include a plaque in Roundhay School, a commemoration in the AJEX Jewish Military Museum and a most impressive 15ft-high bronze statue near the West Yorkshire Playhouse in Leeds.

14

Press on Regardless

William Reid
(3 November 1943)

The tenacious young Scot

A **founding member of the Aircrew Association** and a member of the Victoria Cross and George Cross Association right up to his death in 2001, William 'Bill' Reid was one of the most modest men you could ever wish to meet.

Born in Baillieston, Glasgow on 21 December 1921, Reid was educated at Swinton Primary and Coatbridge Secondary Schools. At 19, Reid decided to join the RAF and, on 28 April 1941 he was accepted into the Volunteer Reserve. His service was deferred until the summer, when he received orders to report to No.7 ITW at Newquay. Selected for pilot training, he sailed across the Atlantic to Canada to serve at No.38 SFTS, Monckton, before being posted to No.2 BFTS, War Eagle Field, Lancaster, California on 2 December 1941. Reid learned to fly the North American AT-6A and Vultee BT-13A during his flying training at War Eagle before he was posted back to England in late July 1942. On 6 August, Reid arrived at No.6 (P)AFU at Little Rissington where he had his first experience of multi-engine flying in the ubiquitous Airspeed Oxford. A posting to 29 OTU at North Luffenham followed on 15 September, where, understandably, Reid expected to begin gathering his first bomber crew. However, Reid was a natural pilot and, instead of being posted to an operational unit, he was retained by the OTU to serve as an instructor on the Wellington.

Reid had been promised that he would be posted to a Lancaster unit but the process did not begin until July 1943 when he was sent to 1654 CU at Wigsley for conversion onto the bomber. Quickly gaining experience on the Lancaster, Reid managed to fly as second pilot during a 9 Squadron raid to Mönchengladbach on 30/31 August. His first operational posting finally came on 5 September when FO W Reid '128838' was sent to 61 Squadron at Syerston, an experienced unit which had been operating the Lancaster from April 1942.

Dependable captain

Reid joined 61 Squadron during a lull in operations and his first sortie with his new unit, to Hannover, did not come until 22 September. Reid was allocated Lancaster Mk III, LM360 'QR-O', one of 15 aircraft from the squadron taking part in a 711-strong force. Despite being reasonably new, LM360 was determined not to climb any higher than 14,000 ft and, in order to complete the operation, Reid wisely decided to jettison the 4,000 lb 'cookie' off the Dutch coast and continue with the remainder of the load at a reasonable height.

Before September was over, Reid flew LM360 to Mannheim, Hannover and Bochum, the last operation reporting more than 400 searchlights around the target. The squadron had a busier October with raids on Hagen, Munich, Kassel, Frankfurt and Stuttgart, plus two more trips to Hannover. After another period without operations from 23 October to 3 November, the next operation would be a big one, this time involving 589 aircraft to Düsseldorf, including eleven from 61 Squadron.

Unfriendly welcome over Holland

Once again flying LM360, Reid was accompanied by his regular crew to Düsseldorf. They were navigator Flt Sgt J A Jeffries RAAF, bomb aimer Flt Sgt L Rolton, flight engineer Flt Sgt J W Norris, wireless operator Sgt J J Mann, mid-upper air gunner Flt Sgt D Baldwin DFM on his second tour of ops, and rear gunner Flt Sgt A F Emerson.

The first of 61 Squadron's contribution to the night's activities took off from Syerston at 1658 hrs and one minute later it was Reid's turn. Turning towards the east coast, the formation gradually gained height as they joined the main stream over the Wash and continued towards the Dutch coast. 'Met' had accurately described the weather as being a thin layer of cloud with cirrus above, combined with superb horizontal visibility. The scene was set for a straightforward run towards Düsseldorf.

As the bomber stream crossed the Dutch coast at 21,000 ft, the experienced air gunners of Reid's crew failed to spot a Bf110 night fighter creep up behind LM360. Before they had chance to respond, the Lancaster was riddled with cannon shells,

The shattered LM360, the day after Reid's unscheduled arrival at Shipdham.

which hit both rear and mid-upper turrets and slammed into the cockpit. Reid's first warning that they were under attack was a flash as the instruments were shattered and the front windscreen exploded in a thousand shards. Reid had been hit by small shards of shrapnel and perspex which luckily did not enter his eyes. Shocked and dazed by what had just occurred, the eye-wateringly cold slipstream brought Reid to his senses and he quickly pulled down his googles to protect his eyes. He could feel blood running down his face and taste it in his mouth but the combined effect of the cold and the slipstream soon negated the flow. Having lost 2,000 ft, the damaged Lancaster was now dangerously lower than the rest of the bomber stream, but Reid continued on, despite a severely damaged port elevator, a distinct lack of serviceable instruments and ruptured hydraulic lines.

After enquires from Jeffries as to how he was, Reid deliberately failed to mention his own injuries so as not to worry his crew, informing them that he was alright to continue on to the target.

Challenging flight home

To keep the Lancaster on an even keel, Reid was forced to apply almost full left rudder because of the damaged elevator. Well aware that he would have to exert

A close-up of the rear fuselage of LM360 clearly showing a multitude of holes caused by the two night fighters, and the open bomb bay doors. Surprisingly, the aircraft was as resilient as its pilot, after being repaired it was allocated to 50 Squadron. It was written off on 11 November 1944 after crash-landing with failing engines at Fiskerton.

this additional pressure for some hours to come, Reid got himself as comfortable as possible. However, just as everything seemed to be settling down, the bomber's vulnerable position was picked up by another night fighter. Only minutes after the first attack, an Fw190 came in from the port beam firing lethal cannon shells directly into the nerve centre of the bomber. Navigator Jeffries was killed instantly after being struck by a single cannon shell in the head and wireless operator Mann, also hit, fell on top of him, seriously wounded. Norris the flight engineer was hit in the left arm and Reid was hit again. Further damage had been caused to both gun turrets, the hydraulic system and the oxygen system had also been rendered unserviceable. Ignoring his own injuries, Norris checked on his pilot, making sure he had an oxygen supply from an emergency bottle. Norris also helped Reid with the controls, as by this time the Lancaster had dropped to 17,000 ft.

The aircraft's compass had been destroyed in the first attack, but despite being barely conscious, Reid decided to continue, completely unaware that his navigator had been killed and his wireless operator lay critically injured. Navigating by the stars, he calmly carried on towards the target which was reached one hour later. As he clamped both his arms around the Lancaster's control column to keep the bomber as steady as possible, Rolton, the bomb aimer, planted the bomb load directly onto the target before leaving his station to assist his pilot. The plight of the bomber was now aggravated by the bomb doors which could not be closed because of the damaged hydraulic system.

Now with Norris and Rolton by his side, Reid turned for home, once again using the stars to navigate. Determined to get his crew home, the physical effort of applying permanent left rudder and wrapping his arms around the control column was taking its toll. However, the sudden effect of an intensive flak barrage at the Dutch coast detracted from his injuries and waning strength, and with great skill Reid managed to negotiate the potentially lethal hail of fire without any further damage to LM360.

It was nearly curtains over the North Sea when all four Merlin engines suddenly stopped. The crew were a little light-headed at this stage as the emergency oxygen supply had long run out, resulting in some very slow reaction times. Norris, who was quietly suffering from his own injury, had forgotten to operate the petrol cocks, something he would have done automatically at his flight engineer's station under less stressful conditions. Soon all four engines reassuringly coughed and spluttered back into life.

With a dwindling fuel load, Reid crossed the Norfolk coast, having decided to make for the long wide runway at Wittering, near Stamford. However, in the meantime, a cone of searchlights appeared, presenting a safe haven to land much earlier than anticipated. Reid circled the lights, flashing his own landing lights to indicate to those below that his aircraft was damaged and he was about to attempt an emergency landing. With little or no hydraulic fluid left in the entire aircraft, the undercarriage had to be pumped down. This final exertion, combined with the increasingly mild conditions as the bomber descended, re-opened Reid's wounds he had suffered several hours earlier.

Reid ordered his crew to prepare for a crash-landing, while Rolton positioned himself directly behind his pilot's seat, ready to pull him away from the controls should he pass out or lose control. Reid was determined not to do either, and as the Lancaster touched down on the unknown but welcoming runway, the main undercarriage collapsed. LM360 scraped along on her belly for less than 100 yards before the whole ordeal was over at precisely 2201 hrs. It was only when the emergency services arrived on the scene that Reid and his crew realised they were on a USAAF station, home of the 44th Bomb Group at Shipdham. Only when his crew were evacuating, did Reid discover that his navigator was dead, his wireless operator was critically wounded and his flight engineer had been injured. All were quickly taken to Shipdham's medical centre, where, sadly, Sgt Mann succumbed to his injuries later the following day.

The remainder of 61 Squadron had all returned safely to Syerston and in the summary of the night's events in the unit's ORB, the following was written, 'Opposition was rather aimless, little heavy flak and a large number of searchlights and few fighters.' I'm sure Reid and his crew would have described a completely different experience.

Recognition

While in hospital, Reid was visited by Air Vice Marshal Cochrane who, after studying all of the reports, recommended that three men should be recommended for gallantry medals. Norris was awarded the CGM, Emerson the DFM, while Reid was awarded, much to his amazement, the VC, which was gazetted on 14 December 1943 and awarded by King George VI at Buckingham Palace on 11 June 1944.

After a period of convalescence, Reid was informed that he would be posted to 617 Squadron, a move which he quietly accepted, while being privately delighted to have been selected for the RAF's elite bomber unit.

In January 1944, Reid joined the unit at Woodhall Spa to serve on 'C' Flight, having been allocated Lancaster Mk I, ME557 'KC-S' as his personal aircraft. Reid flew his first operational sortie for 617 Squadron on 18 April which involved an attack on Juvisy marshalling yards near Paris as part of a series of effective pre-invasion forays. Reid flew his first 'Tallboy' (a 12,000 lb deep penetration bomb) operation to the Samur rail tunnel on 8 June, an operation led by Wg Cdr G L Cheshire DSO, DFC (yet to be awarded his VC). Further 'Tallboy' operations continued throughout the post-invasion period, culminating, for Reid at least, on 31 July when the squadron attacked a 'V' weapon storage base, which occupied a railway tunnel at Rilly La Montagne. Reid managed to drop his 'Tallboy' on target from 12,000 ft, but just seconds later, his Lancaster was struck by a 1,000 lb bomb dropped by another Lancaster from 18,000 ft. ME557 was struck in the middle of the upper rear fuselage, severing the control cables and structurally weakening the aircraft. Reid

Flight Lieutenant Reid, VC (RAF Retired) in company with Barnes Wallis at Scampton in 1967 during the 24th Anniversary celebration of the formation of 617 Squadron. Via RAF Scampton Museum

gave the order to bail out, at which point, the bomber began to enter a dive, pinning him into his seat. Reaching for the upper escape hatch, Reid managed to get out just moments after the Lancaster broke in two, filling the sky with a shower of lethal fragments. Otherwise, only the wireless operator, FO D Luker, managed to escape. One of those who perished was Plt Off L G Rolton DFC, who had served alongside Reid ever since OTU.

Both Reid and Luker served out the rest of the war as POWs, initially at Stalagluft III at Sagan and then at Stalag IV, Belleria. Repatriated in May 1945, Reid was demobbed in January 1946 to resume his pre-war studies in the field of agriculture at Glasgow University and then the West of Scotland Agricultural College. He graduated with a BSc in 1949.

Reid remained in agriculture for his entire working career, including a spell as an agricultural adviser for the MacRobert Trust, Douneside, from 1950. In 1952 he married Violet Campbell Gallagher, who had no idea that he had been awarded the VC during the war. William 'Bill' Reid VC passed away, aged 79, on 28 November 2001 and is buried in Crieff Cemetery, Perthshire.

Against All Odds

Cyril Barton
(31 March 1944)

Lead by example

orn in Elveden, Suffolk, on 5 June 1921, Cyril Joe Barton was raised in New Malden, Surrey by his parents Frederick and Ethel Barton. Educated at Beverley Boys' School in New Malden and later Kingston upon Thames Technical College, Barton was a religious man who lived his life within Christian principles but never forced his beliefs on those around him. On the outbreak of the war, Barton was serving as an apprentice draughtsman in the local Hawker factory, an environment that would have influenced his decision to volunteer for aircrew duties.

Barton enlisted on 16 April 1941 and following the completion of his basic training and promotion to LAC on 1 November, he set sail for the USA to begin his pilot's course. After passing through Maxwell Field in early January 1942, Barton was sent to Darr Aero Technical School, Albany, Georgia on 17 January. Just two days later, he was in the air for the first time in his life, behind the controls of a Boeing PT-17 and, on 20 February, was flying solo. Preliminary flying training was completed on 4 July and Barton was then posted to Cochran Field, Macon for basic flying training until 7 September. He was then sent to Napier Field, Dothan, Alabama for advanced training, where he graduated as sergeant pilot on 10 November 1942.

It was time to sail back to England where, on 15 March 1943, Barton was posted to 6 (P)AFU at Little Rissington. Mainly flying from one of the unit's RLGs at Chipping Norton, Barton was introduced to multi-engine aircraft for the first time thanks to the ubiquitous Airspeed Oxford. A posting to 19 OTU at Kinloss followed on 4 May and it was there, as was traditional, where Barton began to pick his own crew. First was navigator Sgt J L Lambert, then wireless operator Plt Off J Kay, bomb aimer FO G G Crate RCAF and air gunner Sgt F Bryce. This crew flew together for the first time on 1 June in an Armstrong Whitworth Whitley and, for the next few weeks, they were never far apart whether in the air or on the ground. The next stage of training was with 1663 HCU at Rufforth from 17 July and it was here that the final two members of the crew were recruited in the shape of flight engineer Sgt M E Trousdale and air gunner Sgt H C H D Wood. From this stage onwards, the crew referred to their skipper as 'Cy'. It was also at Rufforth that the crew, after two years of training, were introduced to their operational aircraft; the Handley Page Halifax.

No place for slackers

Not long after arriving at Rufforth, Barton was introduced to operational flying with a trip as second pilot on board 76 Squadron Halifax Mk V, DK203 to Hamburg on 24/25 July. Just three nights later, Barton returned to Hamburg, as second pilot, to gain experience. This time he was in Halifax Mk V, DK241, also from 76 Squadron operating from Holme on Spalding Moor. On 1 August, Barton, still as second pilot, flew for the first time in a Halifax with his own crew on board.

Once Barton was in the pilot's seat, he was constantly striving for his crew to be as efficient as possible and he was adamant that there was 'no place for slackers'. In the air, the one rule he would fervently enforce was that there would be no swearing, but on the ground all of his crew were left to their own devices. This did not mean that he did not accompany his crew socially, another policy he would enforce on himself was that he would always buy the first round of drinks for his men before discreetly leaving. Being a teetotaller, Barton would prefer an evening at the cinema rather than the pub.

With their Halifax conversion completed, Barton and his crew were posted to 78 Squadron on 5 September 1943, a unit operating the Halifax Mk II at Breighton. On his arrival, Barton was promoted to flight sergeant and again to pilot officer on 26 September. Following a week of familiarisation training, Barton's crew were ready for their first operation on the night of 15 September, with a raid on the Dunlop rubber factory at Montlues. The reality of how dangerous operations could be was clear on the night of 19 November during an operation to Leverkusen. Barton's Halifax was hit several times by predictive flak which wounded Sgt Lambert and Plt Off Crate. Barton brought the bomber down safely at Woodbridge and both his navigator and bomb aimer made speedy recoveries to re-join the crew for further operations just ten days later.

Barton and his crew were posted to Snaith on 15 January 1944 where, only the day before, 578 Squadron had been formed under the command of Wg Cdr D S S Wilkerson DSO, DFC. The squadron moved and settled at Burn on 6 February and it was from there that Barton was presented with a new aircraft, Halifax Mk III, LK797 'LK-E', which the crew later christened 'Excalibur'. By late March 1944, the crew had become quite attached to LK797 and they decided to chalk an impressive insignia on the nose, complete with the famous sword, pointing vertically through a cloud, its tip resting upon a burning swastika. Sketched out in chalk, the image was waiting its turn to be painted by the local squadron artist but that didn't happen

Out of 6,176 Halifaxes built, 2,091 of them were the Bristol Hercules-powered B Mk III; this variant served with 44 operational squadrons between 1943 and 1945.

before Bomber Command called for another 'maximum effort' to one of the more unpopular targets in Germany, Nuremberg.

Far from ideal conditions

During the morning of 30 March 1944, briefings across the country revealed the target to 795 crews with the promise of high cloud en route to the target and clear conditions over it. That evening would normally have been a moon stand-down period but the senior commanders had decided to work with an early forecast. They chose to ignore an up-to-date weather report presented by a Meteorological Flight Mosquito that showed the chances of protective high cloud was doubtful and that the raid should be cancelled. The scene was now set, and the dice were seriously loaded in favour of the German night fighter force.

The first of 572 Lancasters, 214 Halifaxes and nine Mosquitoes took off at 2116 hrs, to begin the long journey to Nuremburg which was 600 miles into Germany. LK797 'Excalibur' was loaded entirely with incendiaries made up of 48 x 30 lb and 540 x 4 lb bombs. At 2214 hrs, Barton lifted the Halifax away from Burn and on towards the North Sea into a moonlit night with just a few wispy clouds which provided nothing like the cover promised during the briefing. Sgt Bryce in the rear turret later described the trip as 'almost as light as day' and, as the bombers approached the Dutch coast, virtually every aircraft could be seen in the vast stream. Diversions by a handful of aircraft from Bomber Command had been planned but the German fighter controller ignored these and concentrated his forces between a pair of beacons which conveniently straddled the flight path of the Nuremburg force. As the stream approached the Belgian border, the first attacks began and would continue virtually all the way to the target. Barton had managed to escape the attention of the enemy but the tell-tale fighter flares began to get closer as 'Excalibur' was steered towards the last leg of the long flight. The night fighter force had illuminated the bombers with disturbing accuracy, to the point where the aircraft appeared to be flying along a 'runway' of lights, while the enemy selected their victims at will. Barton and his crew, who had seen bombers being attacked, had no idea that

Leading Aircraftsman C C J Barton at Darr Aero Technical School, Albany, Georgia, USA on 20 February 1942; the day of his first solo.

82 aircraft had already been shot down during the outward flight. It was now their turn for some unfriendly attention.

Under attack

After warning his mid-upper and rear turret gunners, Wood and Bryce, to keep their eyes peeled, Barton caught sight of a pair of night fighters approaching directly ahead. Before he had a chance to respond, the white glow of tracer fire, concealing the lethal cannon rounds they were guiding, began to hit 'Excalibur'. The aircraft vibrated and shuddered as the cannon shells slammed into the fuselage, rupturing two fuel tanks, destroying the intercom, disabling the rear turret controls and setting the inner starboard engine aflame as they went. In the rear turret, Bryce spotted what he thought was a Ju88 pass over the Halifax but lost sight of it as Barton began a series of evasive manoeuvres. Moments later, Bryce spotted the same Ju88 coming in for a second attack from the rear but with no intercom to warn his pilot, the rear gunner was forced to use the emergency light button. Holding off just before the Ju88 was about to fire, Bryce signalled to carry out evasive action to starboard while, simultaneously, the rear gunner brought his four .303 machine guns to bear on the enemy. Barton did exactly as requested by his rear gunner but, to his horror, when Bryce pressed the fire button nothing happened.

Barton had done enough to shake off the Ju88 and Bryce signalled again, this time the letter 'R' indicating 'resume course'. However, the Ju88 was determined to finish 'Excalibur' off and suddenly appeared again on the starboard quarter. Bryce signalled to Barton again to carry out evasive action but the Ju88 hit the Halifax again with several rounds tearing through the fuselage. As the fighter banked away, the propeller became detached from the burning engine and Bryce signalled again to resume course. His signal was immediately cancelled out by Sgt Wood in the mid-upper turret, who sent his own signal to Barton for further evasive action, as the same Ju88 attacked again from the port beam. Once again, Barton's skill, combined with excellent teamwork, left the Ju88 frustrated although it did manage a few more strikes on the lower fuselage before it disappeared.

Everything began to settle down again as Barton resumed his original course towards the target. The damaged engine had burnt itself out, the vibration had stopped and the aircraft appeared to be none the worse for wear. However, the German night fighter was determined to have his victory and attacked at high speed from high astern, forcing Bryce to send his all-important signal for further evasive action to his pilot. Barton responded and banked the big bomber over as if it were a fighter which gave Wood the chance to send the Ju88 a burst of fire as it banked away for the final time.

It was at this point that Barton began communicating with his crew to establish if anyone had been hit and how damaged the aircraft really was. He did not get many responses from his crew because in the midst of all the signals being sent and the fighter attacking, three of the crew, Sgt Lambert, FO Crate and Plt Off Kay had bailed out! It had appeared that the three airmen had mistaken Bryce's signals as a 'P' for 'parachute' which simply meant bail out.

It was at this point that many skippers would have made the decision for the remaining crew to bail out as well but instead chose to press on to the target, despite the fact that he had no navigator to guide him and no bomb aimer to drop the bombs. The leaking fuel tanks, a dead engine, lack of intercom and an unserviceable rear turret now seemed like secondary problems.

Following the series of evasive manoeuvres, Barton was not entirely sure where he was but soon approached a large city, which he thought was Nuremburg but later transpired to be more likely Schweinfurt, 50 miles north-west of the intended target (approximately 120 aircraft bombed Schweinfurt by mistake). Single-handedly Barton dropped his cargo of incendiaries and, with little more than a large-scale map strapped to his knee, began the long flight back to Yorkshire.

Long haul home

Aided by the Pole Star, it was not long before 'Excalibur' was over the Dutch coast. Barton had already discussed with Trousdale and Wood whether they wanted to head for Switzerland or make the more arduous flight home. Both opted for home and, once the bomber was over the North Sea, Bryce was able to bring his lonely vigil in his rear turret to an end, and join the remainder of the crew in the front. Barton navigated 'Excalibur' on a northerly course over the great expanse of the North Sea, not realising that at one point they were little more than 20 minutes' flying time from the emergency airfield at Woodbridge in Suffolk. 'Mayday' calls were sent, in the vain hope that the damaged radio could still transmit. Spirits were lifted when a Beaufighter was spotted but, despite using a torch to flash 'SOS' at the aircraft, the machine flew on, completely oblivious to the Halifax. It later transpired that the Beaufighter had been scrambled to intercept an unidentified aircraft and, because the Halifax IFF set was out of action, the 'unidentified' aircraft was in fact Barton's machine. The Beaufighter crew did recognise the aircraft as a Halifax but did not realise that the bomber was the reason for their sortie.

Not long before dawn, Barton, very conscious of the fact that fuel was running low, ordered Trousdale to be prepared at a moment's notice to change fuel tanks when an engine began to cough and splutter. It was then that Barton spotted a light below; at last, after hours over the sea, the aircraft had made landfall. However,

The rear fuselage of Halifax B Mk III, LK797 'LK-E' from which Bryce, Trousdale and Woods emerged to tell the tale. Their brave skipper 'Cy' Barton was not so lucky.

thinking that the Halifax was an enemy bomber, the coastal defences opened fire, forcing Barton to manoeuvre the Halifax back out to sea. Woods plugged in an Alvis lamp and, whilst sitting in the nose, signalled an SOS and a message declaring that they were friendly which brought the firing to an end. As predicted, the engines began to fail and Barton shouted to Trousdale to change tanks. Unfortunately, a piece of shrapnel from the friendly fire had severed the fuel lines and the last few precious gallons of fuel had run out of the bottom of the aircraft. With no time to find an airfield on which to land, Barton ordered Bryce, Trousdale and Wood to prepare for a crash-landing. All three men hunkered down to the rear of the main spar, their hands clasped tightly behind their heads.

This would be Barton's final challenge, to land several tons of aircraft, without power, in low light and on unfamiliar terrain. When just a few feet above the ground, a row of terraced houses in the small colliery village of Ryhope in County Durham, suddenly filled the windscreen, forcing Barton to pull back hard on the control column; a manoeuvre that he could not afford as the airspeed quickly dwindled. Before he could avoid the houses, the starboard wing tore off the chimney pots on the northern side of Hollicarrside Street. Barton was unable to coax the bomber to stay in the air any longer and the port wing dipped down, destroying the end terrace. The Halifax careered through some gardens and greenhouses before crashing into a footbridge over a railway cutting, at which point the bomber broke in two. In the rear section of the aircraft, Bryce, Trousdale and Wood were still huddled together.

All three were alive but injured, Maurice Trousdale most seriously after he took the brunt of the blast from an exploding flap accumulator.

The shattered remains of the forward fuselage still contained Barton who survived the impact of the crash for long enough to ask how the three airmen were, but died 30 minutes later, just before reaching a hospital. The three survivors were helped from the wreckage by a group of miners who gave them first aid and hot sweet tea before they were taken to the Cherry Knowle Hospital. On the ground, one miner, a Mr Heads who was on his way to work, was killed outright on or near the footbridge, and a second miner was injured.

Trousdale, who recovered from his injuries, was awarded an immediate DFM for his efforts that night, while Bryce and Wood received theirs a few weeks later. To their gallant pilot, who was buried in Kingston Cemetery (Class C. (Cons.) Grave 6700) on 6 April 1944, a posthumous VC was awarded on 27 June. The last lines of the VC citation summed up 'Cy' Barton's actions perfectly, 'He lost his life, but the other three members of his crew survived. In gallantly completing his last mission in the face of almost impossible odds this officer displayed unsurpassed courage and devotion to duty.'

16

Just One More 'Op'

Norman Jackson
(26 April 1944)

The role of the flight engineer

Up until 1940, the role of monitoring the temperatures, pressures and fuel of multi-engine aircraft was the responsibility of the pilot, but with the arrival of the four-engine types, beginning with the Halifax, Stirling and later the Lancaster, this task would prove too much for one man. Thus was born a new flying trade, the flight engineer, who would quickly evolve into an integral part of the crew. Only one RAF flight engineer was destined to win Britain's highest accolade, and this was Sgt Norman Cyril Jackson.

Jackson was born in Ealing on 8 April 1919 and as a small child was adopted by Mr and Mrs Edwin Gunter. He had a natural bent for all things mechanical and after leaving school he qualified as a fitter and turner. Already married to Alma and secure in a profession which meant he had no obligation to do military service, Jackson still decided to volunteer for the RAF when the Second World War broke out. He enlisted on 20 October 1939 and, following the completion of courses at Halton and Hednesford, passed out as a Fitter IIE (engines) within Trade Group 1. Jackson was posted to 95 Squadron which was reformed at Pembroke Dock on 16 January 1941 with the Short Sunderland Mk I. On 18 March 1941, the unit relocated to the more exotic Freetown (Fourah Bay) in Sierra Leone, where Jackson settled into an enjoyable tour of duty working with flying-boats and various marine craft.

However, the chance to re-muster as a flight engineer (who were only drawn from qualified Fitter IIEs in Trade Group 1) was too good to miss. After his application was accepted, Jackson returned to Britain in September 1942 to begin six months of training with 27 OTU, Lichfield, continuing at St Athan from March 1943. He was officially re-mustered as a sergeant flight engineer on 14 June and was posted to 1654 HCU, Swinderby from where he was posted on to 106 Squadron at Syerston on 28 July.

Experienced crew

Jackson soon settled into the routine of operational flying and before the squadron relocated to Metheringham in November 1943, the crew, with FO F M Mifflin DFC from Catalina, Newfoundland as skipper, already had 14 sorties under their belts. The navigator was FO F L Higgins, the bomb aimer Flt Sgt M Toft, wireless operator Flt Sgt E Sandelands, mid-upper air gunner Sgt W Smith and rear-gunner Flt Sgt N H Johnson.

On 24/25 April, Jackson completed his 30th operation in Lancaster Mk III, JB664, while the rest of the crew had only flown their 29th (he had flown an extra op for another crew when their flight engineer was unavailable). Jackson was fully entitled to remain on the ground as he was now 'tour expired' but, rather than let his friends down, he decided to do just one more trip. The next raid was a long-haul to Schweinfurt and this operation would be carried out in a factory-fresh Lancaster Mk I, ME669 'ZN-O'.

Eleven Mosquitoes and 206 Lancasters from 5 Group, and nine Lancasters from 1 Group were detailed for the attack on Schweinfurt. Up until recently it had been traditional for 8 Group to carry out the marking of a target but, on 15 April 1944, 627 Squadron was transferred to 5 Group and this raid would be their first since moving to Woodhall Spa from Oakington.

At 2135 hrs, Mifflin took to the air in ME699, gently turning the bomber on a southerly heading in fine conditions as predicted by the Met office. However, a higher than average head-wind was not expected, but like all of the Lancaster skippers on this trip, he was not unduly concerned, expecting everyone else to be over the target at a similar time. When the objective was finally reached, Mifflin found that ME669 was flying on its own; had they slipped behind or were they in front? Regardless, the target was bombed and a course was set for home. Up to this point, the operation had been a 'milk run', the flak was virtually non-existent and night fighters had not been seen in the area.

Fishpond warning radar

It was all too good to be true and, moments after the crew thought they had been ignored by the enemy, Sandelands' voice suddenly filled Mifflin's headset, telling him that the Fishpond warning radar had been activated. The unidentified blip on Sandelands' H2S screen was closing at some rate and Mifflin warned his rear gunner, Johnson, to be ready.

As Sandelands' warnings grew ever stronger, Mifflin pre-empted them, and by then, the 'blip' could only be a night fighter and began to corkscrew the Lancaster. Both Smith in the mid-upper and Johnson in the rear turret caught the briefest glimpse of the enemy machine, both snatching a short burst of fire. The enemy, which turned out to be an Fw190, was far too quick and the next thing the crew knew about it was when cannon shells started slamming into the fuselage. Jackson was thrown to the floor during the commotion but, once he got back to his feet, he quickly rushed to a blister window to see the Fw190 banking away but, more alarmingly, the starboard inner Merlin was in flames. Jackson immediately activated the engine's internal fire extinguisher which momentarily quelled the flames, only for them to erupt again with greater ferocity.

The Lancaster was now in a perilous condition and if the fire continued at the same pace it would not be long before the fuel tanks were reached and the inevitable explosion would follow. It was almost as if the scene had been staged for Jackson, as he had already spent some time discussing the theory of climbing onto a bomber's wing with the bomb aimer. This was his chance to test his own theory, and he said to his pilot, 'I think I can deal with it, Fred', 'How?' replied Mifflin, 'I'll climb out onto the wing with an extinguisher. That'll fix it.' With very few options on the table, Mifflin agreed but also shouted for his crew to prepare to bail out, if Jackson should fail.

Into a 200 mph slipstream

Jackson had clearly planned in his head many times what he would do in the event of such an incident, and in an almost drill-like manner he donned his parachute, stood on the navigator's table, with a fire extinguisher in his battle dress blouse and pulled the ripcord. Higgins and Toft sorted out the parachute lines so that they could be let out steadily, not only to support Jackson, but, in the event of his falling off the wing it would ensure his chute would open quickly. Jackson then opened the upper escape hatch and squeezed himself through, exposing himself to the icy blast of a 200-mph slipstream. After lying prone on top of the fuselage, still firmly holding onto the edge of the escape hatch, Jackson began lowering himself onto the wing root below. Looking towards the burning engine, Jackson searched for a suitable hand-hold and found the leading edge air intake.

Jackson threw himself forward into the slipstream and managed to gain a good grip on the air intake. He was now within an arm's length of the burning engine and, using all his strength to hold on with his left hand, he used his right to reach into his blouse and grab hold of the fire extinguisher. He hit the end of extinguisher hard on the wing to activate it and with great skill pointed it directly into the heart of the flames via a hole in the engine cowling. After a few seconds, the flames began to die down as the contents of the extinguisher did its job. It was now time to regain the fuselage and, as the air intake was his only holding point, this would take some doing. However, at this point, fate took over and Jackson felt the wing suddenly rise as the bomber manoeuvred to port, under attack for a second time, possibly from the same Fw190.

Despite the roaring noise of the engines and the slipstream, Jackson could still hear the sound of cannon fire only seconds before he felt a searing pain in his back and legs. He let go of the fire extinguisher and a sudden gush of flame from the engine erupted over his body. He then lost his grip and was lifted away from the wing, thrown rearwards to a point just behind the rear turret, the smouldering rigging lines of his parachute keeping him there like an out of control kite, buffeted in the slipstream. Back in the fuselage, the crew had already been ordered to bail out but Higgins and Toft were determined to give their flight engineer every chance of survival and both men payed out the rest of his chute before making their own escape.

Jackson was free and alone in the darkness but he was not out of the woods yet because his canopy, as well as the rigging lines of his chute, had caught fire after the engine had burst back into flames for the final time. In desperation, he smothered the flames on the rigging lines with his bare hands, which had already been severely burnt. Despite being damaged, the canopy held firm for a survivable descent. Jackson hit the ground very hard, the pain in his back and legs was now joined by that in his ankles as the flight engineer landed in a heap among some bushes. He did not move for several hours but was conscious enough to realise that he had broken at least one of his ankles in the landing. He was carrying a few shell splinters and shrapnel in his back and legs, not to mention his face that was so burnt one eye could not be opened, while his hands, shrivelled by the flames, were numb.

Harsh treatment

By daybreak on the morning of 27 April, Jackson was in a sorry state but was strong enough to find help, albeit by moving on his elbows and knees. It seemed like an eternity to him as he crawled through the forest he had dropped into before arriving at a small cottage. With just enough strength to knock on the door with his elbow, he was eventually greeted by a hostile German who instantly began a torrent of

Flight Engineer N C Jackson VC outside Buckingham Palace on 13 November 1945 with Group Captain G Cheshire VC.

insults. He was taken inside by a pair of more sympathetic young girls who lived in the cottage but it was not long before the owner had informed the local police. They then made him walk to the nearest town, with only the shoulder of one of the policemen for support; a gesture appreciated by Jackson but his pain by this stage was becoming unbearable. He received some very shoddy first aid treatment at the local hospital before he was paraded through the streets of the town. He was then subjected to a further torrent of abuse by the local population, some of them throwing stones at the unfortunate flight engineer who, by this stage, was slumped in a semi-comatose state and was becoming oblivious to his condition and his treatment.

Jackson spent the next ten months in a German hospital recovering from his injuries before being incarcerated in Stalag IX-C near Bad Sulza, in eastern Germany in February 1945. He was destined not to remain there very long and, after only a

Norman Jackson with his wife Alma in 1945.

few days, made his first escape attempt. His second was more successful and he later reached a US Army unit. By a matter of weeks he avoided the evacuation of the camp and one of the many infamous long marches to escape the advancing Allies.

Repatriation and award

Jackson had no idea that four members of his crew had survived to also become POWs; Higgins, Toft, Sandelands and Smith all escaped the burning bomber but Mifflin and Johnson perished. Once safely back in England, the story of Jackson's incredible attempt to save the aircraft was revealed and, after being promoted to warrant officer, the flight engineer was awarded the VC, gazetted on 26 October 1945. On the day of Jackson's investiture at Buckingham Palace on 13 November 1945, he was accompanied by a group captain who was unknown to him at the time. The individual was Leonard Cheshire who insisted that they should approach the king together. It was then that Cheshire uttered the following words that would remain with Jackson for the rest of his life, 'This chap stuck his neck out more than I did; he should get his VC first.' The king could not break protocol and the senior rank received his award first.

On leaving the RAF, Jackson went on to have six children with his wife Alma and worked as a travelling salesman for Haig Whisky. Norman Jackson passed away at the age of 74 on 26 March 1994 and was laid to rest in the Percy Road Cemetery Twickenham, Middlesex (Section O, Grave No. 181). His VC, which was purchased by Lord Ashcroft for £235,250, is on display in the Lord Ashcroft Gallery in the Imperial War Museum.

The 'Selfless Recipient'

Andrew Mynarski
(13 June 1944)

A furrier from Manitoba

Three Royal Canadian Air Force airmen were destined to win the VC during the Second World War; Andrew Charles 'Andy' Mynarski was the first of them. The oldest son of recently arrived Polish immigrants, Mynarski was born in Winnipeg, Manitoba on 14 October 1916. He was educated at the King Edward and Isaac Newton schools, followed by further education in St John's Technical School. In 1932, his father passed away, leaving Mynarski, aged 16, to support his mother, Anna, and his two brothers and three sisters. At 19, Andy, as he was known to his closest friends, began a career in the fur trade, working as a furrier and chamois cutter, and if the Second World War had not come along, this would have been the young Canadian's future. Mynarski felt that he should contribute to the war effort by joining the Royal Winnipeg Rifles in November 1940 but, for some unknown reason, he only served with them for a short period before returning to his original trade.

Under no obligation to take part in the conflict, Mynarski finally volunteered for the RCAF, enlisting on 29 September 1941. Posted to No.3 Manning Depot, Edmonton, once his initial training was complete, he was sent to No.2 Wireless School, Calgary where he began training as a Wireless Air Gunner on 28 March 1942. Mynarski struggled with the essential Morse code and as a result was posted to No 3 B&GS at Macdonald, Manitoba on 12 September, from where he passed out as an air gunner on 18 December 1942. In January 1943, Mynarski was promoted to sergeant, just before sailing for England where his initial port of call was a Personnel

Reception Centre in Bournemouth, a unit which handled EATS-training air crew.

On 2 March 1943, Mynarski was posted to 16 OTU at Upper Heyford, which was operating Wellingtons, and then completed the final stages of his training with 1661 HCU at Winthorpe, where he was first introduced to the Lancaster on 10 June. It was here that he joined his first crew, not all of whom would have been from his native Canada, and had his first operational posting on 31 October to 9 Squadron, stationed at Bardney. Mynarski, then a flight sergeant, served with 9 Squadron for only a few weeks before he was posted out to 1664 HCU at Croft on 1 December, a unit which operated within 6 Group RCAF specifically to train all-Canadian crews on the Halifax. At Croft Mynarski finally met the men he would go into action with; all of them, with the exception of the

Sergeant A C Mynarski after he qualified as a Wireless Air Gunner in March 1942.

flight engineer, were Canadians. They were pilot, FO A De Breyne; flight engineer Sgt R E Vigars; navigator FO A R Body; bomb aimer Sgt J W Friday; wireless operator W/O II W J Kelly; and FO G P Brophy in the rear turret. The newly-promoted W/O II Mynarski would operate the mid-upper turret.

On 10 April 1944, the crew was posted to 419 (Moose) Squadron at Middleton St George, a unit which was converting from the Halifax Mk II to the Canadian-built Lancaster Mk X.

Building operational experience

Mynarski experienced his first operation with 419 Squadron on the night of 22/23 April during a raid on the railway yards at Laon. Flying in Halifax Mk II, HR925 'VR-D', De Breyne brought the bomber home safely to Middleton. However, Mynarski's crew would fly only one more operation in the Halifax, an aircraft that they had

The man Mynarski so desperately tried to save, rear gunner, Flying Officer George Brophy RCAF.

worked so hard with at the HCU before they were locally converted onto the Lancaster Mk X. Nine Lancasters went into action with the squadron for the first time in a raid on the railway yards at Montzen in Belgium on 27 April 1944. This operation was the last in which the squadron's remaining Halifaxes would take part.

Allocated Lancaster Mk X, KB718 'VR-J', De Breyne took part in an attack on St Ghislain railway yards on 1 May and this was followed by three further operations against railway targets in KB712, KB719 and KB718. Targets in northern France occupied 419 Squadron during May and into June as the build-up to Operation *Overlord* continued. After a period of flying whichever Lancaster was available, early June saw Mynarski's crew allocated their own aircraft in the shape of KB726 'VR-A'. Operations in support of *Overlord* went on, including the biggest show of all, on the night of 5/6 June, when more than 1,000 bombers, dropping 5,000 tons of bombs, attacked coastal batteries and communication targets; for 419 Squadron, the target was Longues. Further raids followed on Coutances and Acheres before a large effort was planned for the night of 12/13 April.

Low-level to Cambrai

On the afternoon of Monday 12 June 1944, 16 crews of 419 Squadron listened intently to their briefing. The target would be the railway yards at Cambrai but, rather than bombing at 20,000 ft, the crews were instructed to bomb from a mere 2,000 ft on to Pathfinder markers. The weather was predicted to be good and with 16 500 lb General Purpose (GP) bombs and a pair of 500 lb GPs with long-delay fuses on board, KB726 took off from Middleton at 2144 hrs.

Once over the French coast, De Breyne began manoeuvring the Lancaster

An impressive bronze statue of Mynarski, by the sculptor Keith Maddison, was dedicated at Middleton St George (now Teesside Airport) in 2005.

towards Cambrai, more than 70 miles ahead. As KB726 closed on the target, intensive flak could be seen while out of sight of De Bryne. The sky was already crawling with night fighters. Moments later, KB726 was subjected to a devastating attack by a Ju88 night fighter from the port beam before it swung round to attack from below and astern only seconds later. Both port engines were knocked out and fire spread quickly through the aircraft, setting hydraulic pipes alight in the rear fuselage and immobilising the rear turret. Brophy still had manual controls but in his efforts to respond to the attack, the winding handle broke off in his hand, trapping the rear gunner inside his turret. De Breyne, realising that his controls were not responding, and with a pair of dead engines, made a snap decision to order his crew to bail out. Mynarski instantly responded to his skipper's order and, as he left his mid-upper turret to leave by the rear door, he noticed that Brophy was trapped inside his rear turret with flames rapidly filling the fuselage from the burning hydraulic fluid. With complete disregard for his own safety, Mynarski rushed to the aid of Brophy, making every effort to free the rear gunner by trying to move the jammed turret with his bare hands. Brophy waved him away, realising that nothing could be done. By then Mynarski's clothing and parachute were well alight and, as a parting gesture, he saluted Brophy as he jumped out of the door.

Several French people saw Mynarski's descent and later reported that both his parachute and clothing were on fire. With barely enough of his flaming parachute intact to slow his descent the brave Canadian hit the ground very hard. He was found by some Frenchmen and, despite their efforts (they had managed to summon a local doctor to attend him) Mynarski quickly succumbed to his burns. Meanwhile, with Brophy still trapped in his turret, KB726 crashed to the ground throwing the rear gunner clear and, along with De Breyne, Friday and Kelly, he managed to evade capture. Brophy later described Mynarski's efforts to save his life, with complete disregard for his own. Mynarski was awarded the most conspicuous award for heroism, a posthumous VC on 11 October 1946, the only such honour bestowed upon a Canadian airman of 6 Group, Bomber Command.

On the day before his last operation, Mynarski was promoted to pilot officer and this is the rank displayed on his grave in the Meharicourt Communal Cemetery, (49°48'12.26"N, 2°43'45.75"E), 20 miles south-east of Amiens. The Lancaster on the cover is painted to represent KB726 and today is actively operated by the Canadian Warplane Heritage. The aircraft was flown across the Atlantic to join the Battle of Britain's Memorial Flight Lancaster during Britain's airshow circuit in August and September of 2014.

Second to None

Leonard Cheshire
(July 1944)

Living life to the full

Of the 51 VCs awarded for aerial operations since 1915, only five were presented to men for carrying out an extended period of operations, and in this group of rare individuals only one earned his VC during the Second World War; namely Geoffrey Leonard Cheshire.

Born in Chester on 7 September 1917, young Geoffrey, forever known as Leonard, was the son of Burella and Geoffrey Chevalier Cheshire, a Professor of Law and a bursar at Exeter College, Oxford. Raised in his parents' home near Oxford, it was from here that Cheshire began his education at the Dragon School, Stowe School and then Merton College, where he studied for a degree in law backed up by a keen interest in languages. It was while studying at Oxford in 1936 that Cheshire entered into a typical young scholar's lifestyle, interested only in drinking, girls and cars, in no particular order.

In 1937 Cheshire first became distracted from his other pursuits by aviation. After joining Oxford University Air Squadron, his first flight was from Abingdon in an Avro Tutor on 5 February 1937 with Flt Lt John Whitworth (later Air Commodore J H H Whitworth who, as a Group Captain, was Station Commander of RAF Scampton during Operation *Chastise*). Cheshire flew solo on 8 June, was commissioned in the RAF VR on 16 November 1937 and then returned to Oxford to continue his studies.

First tour of operations – 102 Squadron

With the outbreak of war, Cheshire was immediately called up for active service. He was ordered to report to 9 FTS at Hullavington, where he received further flying and service training before gaining his RAF wings on 15 December. Promoted to Flying Officer on 7 April 1940, Cheshire was then posted to 10 OTU at Abingdon, where he learnt to fly the Armstrong Whitworth Whitley, before being posted to his first operational unit, 102 (Ceylon) Squadron at Driffield. This squadron, which reformed at Worthy Down in October 1935 with the Handley Page Heyford Mk II and III, re-equipped with the Whitley Mk III in October 1938, and again with the Whitley Mk V in November 1939. It was this variant of the twin-engine bomber that Cheshire would have first encountered at Driffield when he arrived on 6 April 1940.

Cheshire flew his first operation as second pilot on 9 April with Plt Off P H Long DFC, RNZAF, and it was only then that it dawned on him what a responsibility the task of being the skipper was. Cheshire was determined from the outset to show his future crew that he was the best skipper they could wish for, and to do this he would first learn about every single nut and bolt in the aircraft. He even walked through it whilst blindfolded so that he could lay his hand on every crucial component in total darkness. Following a sortie where an engine gave trouble, Cheshire consulted the ground crew, who taught the young pilot as much information about the airframe and the engines as they could, which would prove useful to him in the future.

Cheshire quickly gained operational experience over the coming months against a variety of targets, many of them deep in Germany. His first real test came on the night of 12/13 November 1940, during a raid on an oil refinery at Wesseling, eight miles south of Cologne. For this operation he was at the controls of Whitley Mk V, P5005, 'DY-N', and once he arrived over the target he found it was covered in cloud. Cheshire circled for 50 minutes, before deciding to attack the secondary target, the railway yards at

While the Wellington was famed for the amount of punishment it could take on operations, the Armstrong Whitworth Whitley was an equally tough performer. This is the Whitley Mk V, P5005 which Cheshire and his crew brought home from Cologne on the night of 12/13 November 1940. For his actions that night, Pilot Officer Cheshire was awarded an immediate DSO, and his wireless operator, a DFM.

Cologne. As he settled the Whitley into its bomb run, and with the bomb bay doors open, he prepared to drop a flare. It was at that moment the bomber was shaken by a huge explosion, peppering the aircraft with shrapnel, a small piece of which detonated the flare still inside the bomb bay. With the rear fuselage ablaze, he continued his run, dropped his bombs and then began to assess the damage to his crew and aircraft. The port side of the rear fuselage, a section ten feet long, had been ripped open almost up to the rear access door. The wireless operator was blinded by the explosion but remained at his station, calmly transmitting signals back to base. The rest of the crew managed to put the fire out, while Cheshire settled into the five-hour flight back home to Linton-on-Ouse. After reaching home safely, Cheshire was awarded an immediate DSO, while Harry Davidson, the wireless operator received the DFM.

Second tour of operations – 35 Squadron

After completing his tour with 102 Squadron in January 1941, Cheshire volunteered for a second tour and was posted to 35 Squadron at Linton-on-Ouse. The unit had only been reformed in November 1940 at Boscombe Down, and was the first to receive the Halifax Mk I, one of the RAF's new four-engine 'heavies'. 35 Squadron carried out the first Halifax operation on 11 March 1941, Flt Lt Cheshire carrying out his first 'op' on 15 April, to Kiel. In the meantime, Cheshire had also been awarded a Bar to his DSO for 'outstanding leadership and skill on operations'. Not long after settling into Halifax operations he was detached for ferry duties to Canada and the USA before resuming ops later in the year. Promoted to Squadron Leader on 15 October, he completed his second tour on 22 January 1942.

He was posted to 1652 HCU at Marston Moor as an instructor, but Cheshire still managed to squeeze in four more operations, which included the first '1,000-bomber' raid to Cologne on 30 May 1942.

Third tour of operations – 76 Squadron

From August 1942, Cheshire, now a Wing Commander, became the CO of 76 Squadron, then stationed at Middleton St George, but due to move to Linton-on-Ouse in a few weeks' time. Cheshire proved to be an inspirational leader to the men of 76 Squadron, constantly lecturing his crews to improve their chances of hitting the target and returning home safely.

At the age of 25, Cheshire was promoted to Group Captain and posted to Marston Moor on 1 April 1943 as Station Commander, the youngest officer in the RAF to achieve this. It was a sad moment for 76 Squadron, and the following was written in the unit diary, 'What the squadron has lost Marston Moor will gain. It is under the character and personal supervision of Group Captain Cheshire that the squadron became what it is today – one of the best in Bomber Command.'

Gp Capt Cheshire did not take to his new non-operational role particularly well; the bomber pilot felt completely lost in the world of administration and mediocre duties. He attempted to throw his heart and soul into the job by improving the efficiency of the unit, but when the opportunity to return to operational flying came in September 1943, he grabbed it. He would have to drop back down to the rank of Wing Commander for his new posting, as the CO of none other than 617 Squadron. Only formed in March 1943 specifically for Operation *Chastise*, Cheshire would become its fourth commanding officer when he took up the position in November.

Fourth tour of operations – 617 Squadron

While enthusiastic about his new posting, Cheshire was disappointed to discover that his orders were to train the squadron in high-level bombing techniques. He was not an advocate of this method of attack, having always taken on a target at low level whenever possible. However, he did as ordered until 8 February 1944 when 617 Squadron was finally called to arms again with an attack on the Gnome-Rhône factory in Limoges. The unit was under strict instructions to only hit the factory because of the proximity of French workers' homes. Cheshire seized the opportunity to prove that true accuracy could only be achieved at low level. At the controls of a Lancaster, Cheshire dropped target markers directly onto the factory from just 200 ft and the resulting bombing was delivered with equal accuracy, causing no casualties in the local population.

Clearly Cheshire's theory had worked and he was supplied with a Mosquito as his personnel marker aircraft. Several specialist targets were attacked by 617 Squadron over the next few weeks, from the Michelin rubber factory at Clermont-Ferrand to the Antheor viaduct in Italy; the latter unsuccessfully involving 12,000 lb High Capacity 'blockbuster' bombs. Further Mosquitoes were supplied to 617 Squadron specifically for low-level target marking duties as it became clear to senior staff that Cheshire's method worked. Always leading the squadron from the front, Cheshire continued to improve the technique of marking and using a master bomber. A good example of this was the highly successful attack on the 21st Panzer Division at Mailly-le-Camp on 4 May 1944. The marking and subsequent bombing saw the demise of almost 20,000 troops in a classic example of tactical bombing.

Another of 617 Squadron's successful operations was in support of Operation *Overlord* on 8/9 June 1944 which saw the debut of the 12,000 lb Tallboy, also

A smiling Leonard Cheshire in tropical uniform, most likely during his service in India in late 1944.

nicknamed the 'earthquake bomb'. The target was the Saumur railway tunnel which was the German's main supply line to the southern region of Normandy. 617 Squadron fielded 19 Lancasters carrying Tallboys and a further six with conventional bombs led by Cheshire in a Mosquito. With outstanding precision, Cheshire dropped his markers just 40 yds from the south-western entrance of the tunnel, not to mention the markers that were dropped accurately by the Pathfinder unit, 83 Squadron. The subsequent downpour of Tallboys saw the total destruction of the tunnel and at least one of the 'deep penetration' weapons sliced through the hillside and exploded within the railway tunnel.

From June to September 1944, 617 Squadron became heavily involved in Operation *Crossbow* which was to destroy the V-1 and V-2 weapons. 617 Squadron's first involvement in *Crossbow* was on 25 June 1944, when they were ordered to attack the V-1 storage bunker at Siracourt. On the morning of the attack, a crate containing a P-51 Mustang was delivered to Woodhall Spa as a personal gift to Cheshire from the US 8th Air Force. The aircraft was quickly assembled and despite the fact that it had not been flight tested, and that Cheshire had not flown a single-engine aircraft for four years, he set off to lead his squadron to Siracourt. Cheshire marked the target with his usual accuracy and then, having returned to Woodhall Spa, landed the unfamiliar fighter in the dark without difficulty.

On 6 July 1944 Cheshire completed his 100th operational sortie. On his return he was interviewed by the AOC 5 Group, Air Vice Marshal R A Cochrane who informed him that he would be rested from operations. Cochrane had also recommended that Cheshire be awarded the VC which was gazetted on 8 September 1944.

The 103rd operation

On 10 September 1944, having been promoted back up to Group Captain, Cheshire left England bound for India, where he would take up a position in the Eastern Air Command HQ in Calcutta. By late 1944 he was in the USA working for the British Joint Staff Mission in Washington, specialising in the study of tactical developments. While he was in Washington he was selected as a British observer for the second atomic bomb raid against Japan by the USAAF. At the end of July he was sent to Guam and then on to Tinian Island, the B-29A Superfortress base from where the raid would take place against Nagasaki.

On 9 August 1945, Cheshire boarded the support B-29A, named 'Big Stink' flown by Capt J Hopkins; this would be Cheshire's 103rd and final operation. A failure by Hopkins to rendezvous with two other B-29s over Yakushima meant that Cheshire did not witness the detonation from as close as intended, but it was close

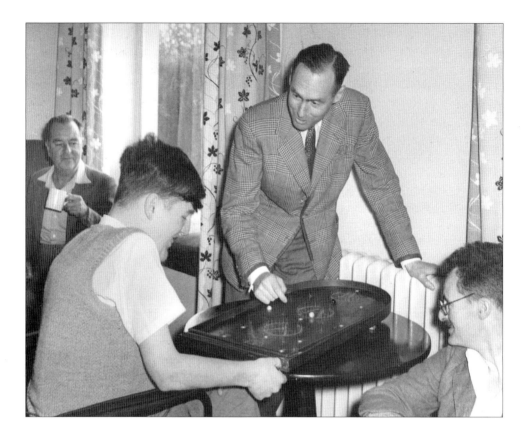

Leonard Cheshire visiting one of the many ex-servicemen's homes. Today the organisation is called Leonard Cheshire Disability, a global network which has over 200 independently managed Cheshire partner organisations in 54 countries.

enough to realise how devastating the effects of an atomic weapon were. On his return to England, Cheshire was ordered to report what he had witnessed at Nagasaki to the British Prime Minister, Clement Attlee.

After attending a Medical Board in late 1945, Cheshire was informed that he was suffering from psychoneurosis and as a result he requested a medical discharge from the RAF which was granted in January 1946.

Legacy

After leaving the RAF, Cheshire entered into several ventures but it was to The Cheshire Foundation Homes for the Sick (today known as the Leonard Cheshire

Disability) founded in 1948 that he dedicated the rest of his life. Cheshire met Sue Ryder in the mid 1950s, a woman who had experienced war in a similar fashion and who was equally prepared to spend the rest of her life helping others. The couple married on 5 April 1959 and together they set up the Ryder-Cheshire Foundation which helped to rehabilitate disabled people, and raised money for the prevention and treatment of tuberculosis.

Cheshire was made a Member of the Order of Merit in 1981, and in 1991 became a Baron as a result of his extensive charity work. Group Captain Geoffrey Leonard Cheshire VC, OM, DSO and Two Bars, passed away on 31 July 1992 and is buried in the village of Cavendish in Suffolk. His impressive medals, which also include the 1939-45 Star, Air Crew Europe Star, Burma Star, Defence Medal, Queen Elizabeth II Coronation Medal (1953) and Queen Elizabeth II Silver Jubilee Medal (1977) are on display in the Imperial War Museum, London.

With the Pathfinders

Ian Bazalgette
(4 August 1944)

Engineering pedigree

Ian Willoughby Bazalgette, the great-grandson of the civil engineer Sir Joseph Bazalgette, who was instrumental in establishing a network of sewers under the streets of London, was born in Calgary, Alberta on 19 October 1918. His parents, Charles and Marion were English and Irish-born respectively. Bazalgette's education began in Toronto Balmy School but when the family moved to England in 1927 and settled in New Maldon, he attended Rokeby Preparatory School and then Beverley Boys' Secondary School. At the tender age of 13, Bazalgette was struck down with tuberculosis which resulted in a spell from August to December 1931 in the Royal Sea-Bathing Hospital in Margate.

Bazalgette's military career began on 16 July 1939 when he joined the Royal Artillery, gaining the rank of Second Lieutenant on 7 September 1940. He first served with a Searchlight Section, then as an instructor in Scotland, but the job was clearly not what he had hoped for and he wanted to be much closer to the action. He transferred to the RAF and was sent to Cranwell for pilot training on 13 September 1941. Within a week he had flown solo. He was promoted to Pilot Officer, RAFVR on 24 January 1942, and then posted to 25 OTU at Finningley for further instruction. On 15 September 1942, his training now complete as a bomber pilot, Bazalgette was posted to 115 Squadron, equipped with Wellingtons at Mildenhall.

Squadron Leader Ian Willoughby Bazalgette, a brave pilot described by his navigator Geoff Goddard as 'an excellent pilot, cool, efficient, with the capacity to inspire confidence in all who flew with him.'

115 Squadron

Bazalgette flew his first operation, a 'gardening' sortie on 30 September 1942, and by the end of November had already accumulated twelve operations. At the same time, 115 Squadron began converting to the Hercules-powered Lancaster Mk II, and the unit withdrew from operations as new crews and aircraft began to arrive. It was not until 22 March 1943 that Bazalgette flew his first Lancaster operation, in DS615, 'KO-N', to St Nazaire, only to be recalled before reaching the target.

Bazalgette quickly settled into Lancaster operations, although on his first full sortie to Duisburg on 26 March, the bomber was hit by flak which resulted in a belly-landing back at base. Raids to Berlin and Essen followed and in early April, his 'determination and skill on operations' was rewarded with the DFC on 29 May 1943. Promotion to Squadron Leader followed on 12 June and on 12 August, flying DS664, 'KO-X', to Milan, Bazalgette finished his tour of operations. He was sent on 'post-operational' leave and was told to wait for news of his next posting, which would undoubtedly be an instructor's job. The idea of spending the remainder of his career at an OTU did not inspire him, but an earlier visit by 8 Group's Wing Commander 'Hamish' Mahaddie to 115 Squadron had made quite an impression on Bazalgette. After presenting a lecture on Pathfinder techniques, Mahaddie suggested to Bazalgette that he should apply for a transfer to 8 Group once his tour of duty was complete. Bazalgette did just that, but a higher power had other ideas and his application was rejected, as an OTU instructor wanted to join 115 Squadron. As a result Bazalgette was posted to 20 OTU at Lossiemouth to become the unit's 'C' Flight Commander.

During his tour of duty at Lossiemouth, Bazalgette met FO Douglas Cameron DFM, who was serving as the OTU's gunnery leader. Cameron was Plt Off Ron Middleton's mid-upper gunner and when Bazalgette left Lossiemouth on 20 April 1944, he chose the ex-149 Squadron man as his regular rear gunner for his new operational crew.

'We lead, others follow'

Bazalgette's return to operations was a posting to the recently formed Pathfinder unit, 635 Squadron at Downham Market with Lancasters. Formed on 20 March 1944 from flights donated by 35 and 97 Squadrons, this latest 8 Group unit had pedigree from the outset. After attending a PFF conversion course at Warboys,

635 Squadron Lancaster ND898 'K for King' parked in the Oak Woods dispersal at Downham Market in late 1944. The bomber is displaying 27 operation symbols under the cockpit.

Bazalgette carried out his first operation with 635 Squadron on 6 May in Lancaster ND895, when he dropped twelve 1,000 lb bombs on the marshalling yards at Mantes Gassicourt. May was dominated by pre-invasion operations and on 6 June

1944 Bazalgette, in Lancaster ND950, 'F2-M', bombed the shore batteries at Longues. The following day he bombed an ammunition dump at Fôret de Cerisy and on 9 June, the Luftwaffe airfield at Rennes saw Bazalgette deliver a neat line of 18 500 lb bombs across the runway. He was nominated as Deputy Master Bomber for an attack on the railway yards at Cambrai on 12 June, flying ND821 as one of the first marker aircraft. Back at the controls of his regular Lancaster, ND950, he was again Deputy MB for a raid on the railway yards at Lens.

Operation *Crossbow* began in late June with 635 Squadron making its first contribution on 23 June with an attack on a V-1 site at Coubronnes, followed the next day by a similar raid on a site at Le Grand Rossignolle. Bazalgette flew another six operations during August, which included enemy troop concentrations, railway yards and more V-1 sites; he was employed to mark or illuminate the target. On 20 July, Bazalgette took the role of MB for the first time in a daylight raid on the V-1 site at L'Hey, while the end of the month saw a return to strategic operations with targets in Germany back on the agenda. On 30 July, he served as MB again for a raid in support of Allied invasion forces and as Deputy MB for a daylight raid on Chappel Notre Dame on 1 August.

The month began as the previous one had ended, with more attacks on flying-bomb and storage sites, all of which were generally successful. These operations were seen as almost routine but one in particular stands out above the rest because of the actions of Sqn Ldr Bazalgette on 4 August. For this operation he was allocated Lancaster Mk III, ND811, 'F2-T'. His crew were Flt Lts G Goddard (navigator), I A Hibbert (bomb aimer) and C R Godfrey DFC (wireless operator) all of whom had joined Bazalgette at Lossiemouth and joined 635 Squadron together, along with Douglas Cameron (rear gunner). Sgt G R Turner joined the crew when they arrived at Downham Market, while the mid-upper gunner, Flt Sgt V V R Leeder RAAF was only on loan for this operation.

Target Trossy-St-Maximin

The attack was against the flying-bomb storage sites at Bois de Cassan and Trossy-St-Maximin and involved 291 aircraft from 6 and 8 Groups. The site at Trossy had only been bombed a few days earlier and the local flak crews were more than ready if Bomber Command dared to return. The 61 Lancasters from 8 Group, led by MB, Wing Commander D W S Clark, had a rough ride on approaching the site and, of the 14 crews from 635 Squadron who took part, eight were damaged by flak before a bomb was dropped. Clark's aircraft was raked by anti-aircraft fire along the length of the fuselage but he was lucky to get away with only a damaged elevator. The Deputy MB, Flt Lt R W Beveridge DFC and crew in Lancaster Mk III, PA983, 'F2-A' were not so lucky. They took a direct flak hit, burst into flames and nose-dived into the ground near the target, killing all eight on board.

Then it was Bazalgette's turn and he was determined to plant his markers on target, but the defenders had put up a thick wall of flak which he had to fly through if he was to succeed. ND811 was hit by a heavy barrage as he neared the target. Both starboard engines were knocked out and the starboard wing and fuselage were set on fire. Hibbert, the bomb aimer, came off worst in the onslaught; he lost an arm and part of his shoulder blade, while Leeder in the mid-upper turret was overcome by fumes in the smoke-filled fuselage. Hibbert's condition was poor but he was carried to the rest bunk and given morphine while the rest of the crew tried to fight the flames in the fuselage. In the rear of the bomber, Cameron turned his turret to beam and was shocked to see that the starboard wing was already burnt down to the framework and he was equally alarmed by the sight of fuel pouring along the bottom of the fuselage towards him.

Bazalgette still managed to maintain sufficient control of the bomber to drop his markers on target but just as he did so, the Lancaster entered a spin. Bazalgette regained control and flew the seriously damaged bomber for another 30 miles before a port engine seized, giving Bazalgette no choice but to order 'abandon aircraft'. His crew were concerned about the condition of Hibbert and Leeder, but Bazalgette assured them that he would try to crash-land. Four of his crew, Cameron, Goddard, Godfrey and Turner bailed out safely at 1,000 ft.

It was at this point that the people in the French village of Senantes saw the burning bomber approaching. The Lancaster veered away to avoid the village before Bazalgette carried out an excellent crash-landing in a nearby field. All seemed well until, seconds later, the bomber exploded, killing the three airmen still on board instantly. The remains of Bazalgette were quickly recovered by the locals, while the Germans took the bodies of Hibbert and Leeder away. The four survivors who had bailed out were all hidden from the Germans by the Resistance and they managed to remain out of enemy hands until the Allied forces arrived. It was only then that the villagers of Senantes could give the brave Canadian pilot the burial he deserved on 8 October 1944. Bazalgette's sister, Ethel, attended the funeral as well as the whole village who turned out to honour Bazalgette, Hibbert and Leeder. The Mayor of Senantes later wrote a letter of sympathy to the pilot's mother. When the crew arrived back in England, the story of Bazalgette's final flight was told and he was awarded the highest accolade, the Victoria Cross, gazetted on 17 August 1945. This was the first VC earned by a member of 8 Group.

'Oboe' VC

Robert Palmer
(23 December 1944)

'Man of Kent'

Robert **Anthony Maurice Palmer was born** in Gillingham on 7 July 1920, the son of ex-Royal Flying Corps pilot, Arthur Robert Palmer and Lillian. Educated at Gravesend County School and later Gordon's School, Palmer was fascinated by his father's exploits during the First World War and it was not long before the young man was solely interested in all things aviation. When he left school he was employed in the Borough Surveyor's Department in Gravesend, but with the next conflict rapidly approaching, the 19-year-old enlisted in the RAF on 22 August 1939. The following day he was promoted to Sergeant and on 25 September he began his training at 3 ITW, Hastings followed by basic flying instruction at 7 EFTS at Desford. He arrived at 12 FTS, Grantham on 8 June 1940, later graduating as Sergeant Pilot on 7 September and then moving to 15 OTU at Harwell. With his training finally complete, Palmer was posted to 75 (New Zealand) Squadron on 16 November 1940. He was destined to serve with the Kiwi squadron for only ten days, during which time he flew three operations as second pilot, before being posted again to 149 Squadron at Mildenhall on 26 November. It was with 149 Squadron that Palmer completed his first tour of operations and on 13 February 1941 he was posted to 'C' Flight, 20 OTU, Lossiemouth as an instructor.

Experienced instructor

Palmer was promoted to Flight Sergeant on 1 June 1941 and on 29 January 1942 he was commissioned as a Pilot Officer. He was thoroughly frustrated by his long tour of duty as an instructor, and by the continuous rejection of his applications to return to operations. He did, however manage to fly on all three of Harris' 1,000-

Squadron Leader Robert Anthony Maurice Palmer DFC and Bar who was posthumously awarded the Victoria Cross on 23 March 1945 for his actions on 23 December 1944.

bomber raids which were heavily bolstered by aircraft supplied by OTUs flown by experienced instructors. Palmer was promoted to Flying Officer on 29 January 1942, and again to Flight Lieutenant on 28 December 1942.

A chance to return to flying operations finally came when Sqn Ldr Bazalgette DFC became 'C' Flight Commander of 20 OTU. Bazalgette was in the same position and was totally sympathetic to Palmer's efforts to get back on 'ops'. Supporting his latest application, Bazalgette pointed out that Palmer had by then, been carrying out instructor duties for nearly three years and had accumulated 1,400 flying hours in the process. It is not clear whether Bazalgette's supportive footnotes to Palmer's application helped, but on 9 November 1943, he left Lossiemouth to join the Pathfinder Force. Posted to the Mosquito training unit at Warboys, he finally returned to an operational unit on 16 January 1944 – the Mosquito-equipped 109 Squadron at Marham.

Mossie 'ops' with the Pathfinders

109 Squadron was the first of several Mosquito units to serve with the Pathfinders thanks to its pioneering use of *Oboe*. The ground-breaking radar aid was another addition to Bomber Command's armoury to improve navigation and bombing accuracy. While 109 Squadron and its twin-engine light bombers were a world away from those Palmer had experienced when flying the Wellington, he quickly settled into operations, flying his first on 3 February 1944 when he dropped four 500 lb bombs on Krefeld.

On 1 April the squadron moved from Marham to Little Staughton, an airfield which it shared with another Pathfinder unit, the Lancaster-equipped 582 Squadron, formed there the same day from the 'C' Flights of 7 and 156 Squadrons. The AOC of 8 Group, Air Commodore Don Bennett's long term plan for his Pathfinders was that it would become an all-Mosquito and Lancaster force, and Little Staughton was a good example of his plan finally coming to fruition.

Palmer was awarded the DFC on 30 June 1944, and having already completed his second tour of operations continued to his 100th, for which he received a Bar to

his DFC on 8 December. On 10 December he was promoted to Squadron Leader, but rather than call it a day and see the rest of the war out behind a desk, Palmer chose to stay with 109 Squadron.

On 16 December 1944, the German forces began their final and successful counter-attack through the Ardennes region of Belgium under the code-name Operation *Watch* on the Rhine (aka 'the Battle of the Ardennes' or 'the Battle of the Bulge'). General Eisenhower called on Bomber Command to attack the many communication lines supporting the German offensive, including road junctions and

Robert Palmer (right) during his flying training at 7 EFTS, Desford, in 1940.

Flight Lieutenant G Russell, DFC, Palmer's usual navigator who was one of six aircrew killed in Lancaster Mk III, PB371 on 23 December 1944. Only the rear gunner, Flt Sgt R K Yeulatt RCAF, managed to bail out to become a POW.

railway installations. One of these targets was the Gremberg marshalling yards in Cologne and an attack on the installation was planned for 20 December by units from 8 Group, but it was postponed because of poor weather.

Master Bomber

The raid on Gremberg was re-scheduled for 23 December; a daylight operation to be led by Sqn Ldr Palmer in the role of Master Bomber. Palmer decided to lead the operation at the controls of 582 Squadron Lancaster, PB371, '6O-V' using his own regular Mosquito navigator, Flt Lt G Russell DFC and an experienced crew. These were Flt Lt O S Milne (second pilot), Sqn Ldr A L Carter DFC (second navigator), Flt Sgt B Nundy (signals operator), FO W Dalgarno (mid-upper gunner) and Flt Sgt R K Yeulatt RCAF (rear gunner).

On the morning of 23 December, a small force of 27 Lancasters and three Mosquitoes, all from 8 Group, left Bourn (105 Squadron), Graveley (35 Squadron) and Little Staughton (109 and 582 Squadrons) to attack the marshalling yards in Cologne, led by Palmer who took off from Little Staughton at 1027 hrs, on his 110th operation. The aircraft were divided into three formations, each led by an *Oboe* Lancaster with a 109 Squadron *Oboe* Mosquito Mk XIV, ML998 flown by FOs E C Carpenter RCAF and W T Lambeth DFM, flying close behind Palmer's aircraft. The raid did not get off to a good start as two 35 Squadron Lancaster Mk IIIs, PB678 and PB683, collided at 10,000 ft over the South Foreland, on the Kent coast, at 1133 hrs. All 14 aircrew were lost although it is claimed that some managed to escape by parachute into the sea only to die of exposure before help arrived.

Once the remaining 28 aircraft reached the target, the forecasted 10/10ths cloud at 10,000 ft over Cologne had cleared and, rather than risking a long *Oboe* run in, all aircraft were ordered to break formation and bomb visually. Flying at just 17,000 ft, the flak began to take its toll on Palmer's Lancaster and having failed to receive the break formation order, he continued on the planned *Oboe* course to the target. Flak tore into Palmer's aircraft, setting two engines on fire which quickly spread through the fuselage, setting the bomb-bay ablaze. Palmer knew that during this type of attack, the formation only released their bombs when the lead aircraft did. Maintaining his course, Palmer released his bombs when the signal was received from the ground station and his bombs were seen to land on the marshalling yards. Seconds later, Palmer lost control and PB371 spiralled into the target area in a flaming spiral from which there was no escape. Only the rear gunner, Yeulatt, managed to bail out to become a POW. Behind Palmer's aircraft, Carpenter and Lambeth were also taking damage to their Mosquito. With one engine feathered,

Carpenter had four enemy fighters on his tail but knew that he could not drop his bombs early. After dropping its bombs, ML998 also spiralled down in flames; neither escaped with their lives.

The 8 Group formation found themselves up against part of a force of 250 German fighters that had been sent to attack an 8th Air Force raid. Before the action was over, three more Lancasters had been shot down, all from 582 Squadron, with the loss of another nine men, although twelve survived to become POWs. Two of those POWs were FO H E Parratt DFM and Flt Sgt R K Shirley who were trapped in Lancaster Mk III, PB141 after it entered a flat spin at 20,000 ft and crashed into the marshalling yard they were bombing.

Several other bombers were damaged by flak and were shot up by fighters, including those belonging to Wg Cdr J H Clough and Capt E Swales, who both had running battles with Fw190s and Bf109s. But the day went to Sqn Ldr Palmer who was awarded the highest accolade, a posthumous VC on 23 March 1945, becoming the only *Oboe* VC of the Second World War. Palmer was initially buried in Hoffnungsthal village cemetery but was re-interred after the war, in Rheinberg War Cemetery (Joint grave 14.C. 13-14) with his crew.

On 18 December 1945, Palmer's father, Arthur, received his eldest son's award at an investiture at Buckingham Palace.

Putting your Life on the Line

George Thompson
(1 January 1945)

From greengrocer's apprentice to wireless operator

George **Thompson was born in the beautiful** Scottish county of Perthshire, just north of Auchterarder on 23 October 1920, to James and Jessie Thompson. The family later moved to Glencraig and, it was from there that young George began his education in Portmoak Primary School and then Kinross High School. At 15, Thompson left school to become an apprentice greengrocer in Kinross, an exercise which he took four years to complete before he was declared qualified. By the time he had completed his long apprenticeship, the Second World War had begun, which instantly drew all his attention away from the trade of greengrocer. Determined to do his bit, Thompson's first taste of military service was with the Local Defence Volunteers but he had already set his sights much higher and, in July 1940, decided to enlist in the RAF.

Thompson was only offered deferred service but, rather than wait for the red tape machine to eventually churn out his name, he volunteered again before the year was over, and this time he took a punt at aircrew. On 7 January 1941, Thompson sat before an aircrew selection board but was not taken on. Three days later, determined not to be ignored, he applied for ground crew and was finally accepted.

Thompson chose the RAF wireless trade because he had been very keen on all things pertaining to radio and wireless during his childhood. He successfully passed out of his course in October 1941 and served for a short while at Coningsby before heading overseas to Iraq on 11 February 1942. The tasks he was assigned to during his tour of duty in the Middle East were not particularly challenging and Thompson quickly became bored. To escape this rather mundane world, he once again volunteered for flying duties and, with the demand for aircrew in full swing, he was accepted. By August 1943 he was back in England. He naturally began training as an air wireless operator at No.4 Radio School, Madley, graduating on 29 November as a sergeant wireless operator/air. After completing an air gunnery course, he was posted to 14 OTU, Market Harborough, equipped with the Wellington, where he would find a crew to join.

As with most wireless operators, who were spotted by keen-eyed future skippers long before they were given any chance to pick and choose for themselves, Thompson was recommended to ex-New Zealand farmer, FO R F H Denton RNZAF, by his recently recruited navigator, Flt Sgt E Kneebone. Denton had already recruited a bomb aimer, in the shape of FO E R Goebel, and it was Thompson's turn to be invited to join the Kiwi's crew. With only a pair of air gunners to shop for, Denton chose two Welshmen; 30-year-old Sgt E J Potts as the mid-upper, and Sgt J T Price in the 'tail-end Charlie' position. The six men steadily gelled as a team and, after 80 hours of flying in the Wellington, Denton and his crew were posted to 1654 HCU at Wigsley, where they learned to fly the Stirling. It was there that, as with all HCUs, the seventh member of the crew was 'acquired' – Sgt W N Hartshorn filling the role of flight engineer. Having cut their teeth on a four-engine 'heavy', Denton and crew were put through a short conversion course on the Lancaster and, on 9 September 1944, were posted to 9 Squadron at Bardney.

Hogmanay on hold

Denton and his crew made their operational debut on 6/7 October 1944, in Lancaster Mk III, LM548, on a trip to Bremen, which was the last of 32 major Bomber Command raids on this long-suffering city. Only two further operations were flown during October; one to attack gun batteries near Flushing, and the other against Nuremburg. All was quiet during November, and Denton and his crew would not be called on again until 4 December, when they flew Lancaster Mk I, NG249, to Heilbronn. It was a crushing raid on the town which had not been bombed before and it was equally sobering for the attackers, as a dozen Lancasters failed to return; none of them from 9 Squadron.

Christmas 1944 was enjoyed by the personnel of 9 Squadron and an equally enjoyable event was planned for New Year's Eve. Thompson, being a proud Scotsman, was making the most of Hogmanay when the evening's entertainment was interrupted by the tannoy. The message was that ten crews, Denton's included, should report to the briefing room immediately. Once there, the crews were presented with the target – another attack on the Dortmund-Ems Canal; this time, near Ladbergen.

Accurate flak

For this operation, Denton was allocated Lancaster Mk I, PD377 'WS-U', which was loaded with a dozen 1,000 lb medium capacity long-delay bombs. After being woken from their beds at 0500 hrs, breakfast and a final briefing were carried out before the crews were transported to the frost-covered bombers. PD377 would be the first of the ten 9 Squadron bombers to take off and, at 0744 hrs, Denton opened the throttles, making full use of virtually all of Bardney's main runway before becoming airborne. Three minutes behind, FO C S Newton RCAF in Lancaster Mk I, NG252, thundered down the same runway, only for both port engines to fail just a few moments after take-off, sending the bomber plunging into the ground; only one airman survived. The crew of Lancaster Mk I, PB368 behind, must have looked on with horror as they began their take-off at 0750 hrs. Incredibly, PB368 also crashed just after take-off but this time only one of the crew was injured; it was not an encouraging start for 9 Squadron.

Denton had witnessed the chaos on the ground at Bardney as he steadily climbed away and fully expected to be the only 9 Squadron aircraft to take part in this all-5 Group raid. Seven other squadron aircraft did manage to take off safely but Denton decided to fly on independently, eventually picking up the bomber stream of more than 100 Lancasters and two Mosquitoes over northern France. Settling down at just 10,000 ft, Denton flew a loose formation with an unknown group of Lancasters before making his final run-in to the target with an increasingly clear sky. With Goebel settled into his bomb aimer's position, the first of the dozen 1,000 lb bombs fell away towards the banks of the canal. The flak began to build as they approached the target and one aircraft from 467 Squadron was struck but managed to continue with difficulty. Another bomber was not so lucky, 9 Squadron's own Lancaster Mk I, NG223, flown by FO P W Reaks was hit by flak and only three of the crew managed to escape before the bomber hit the ground.

Just as Denton was about to change course back to England, there was an almighty explosion in front of his aircraft which temporarily rendered the New Zealander unconscious. A flak shell had shattered PD368's nose compartment, smashing open the aircraft's upper cockpit canopy while shards of shrapnel had entered the port inner engine which burst into flames. Only a fraction of a second earlier, another flak shell slammed into the lower rear fuselage, below the mid-upper turret, severing the trimming controls and splitting hydraulic lines as it went. Seconds after the shrapnel had done its damage, the rear fuselage burst into flames, spurting burning hydraulic fluid over Sgt Potts in his mid-upper turret and this was fuelled by the slipstream entering the shattered cockpit canopy.

Denton could only have been knocked senseless for a few moments because he reacted quickly to the burning engine and selected the appropriate fire extinguisher which quickly did its job. With the lifeless Merlin now feathered, Denton concentrated on retaining control, with his foot pressed hard to maintain the starboard rudder to counteract the lack of power on the port side, and with the control column pushed forward to prevent the bomber from stalling. The chances of Goebel, who was still in the bomb-aimer's position, surviving the impact and subsequent explosion of an 88 mm flak shell were slim but, much to the relief of Denton, he emerged from the forward compartment, singed but none the worse for wear, holding the remains of his parachute.

Rescue without hesitation

Positioned between the two flak hits, Flt Sgt Thompson was sitting at his wireless set, totally unscathed. He could clearly see the fire burning to the rear of the aircraft and the perilous position in which both the mid-upper and rear gunners now found themselves. Without thinking, Thompson, who was not burdened with heavy clothing or a parachute, and never wore gloves so that he could use the wireless set easily, stood up and began heading towards the inferno that was engulfing Sgt Pott's turret. A tall man, Thompson was able to straddle the gaping hole caused by the flak, which was just in front of the mid-upper turret, by clinging onto the edge of the damaged fuselage with the tips of his fingers and toes. By the time Thompson arrived at the turret, Potts was unconscious and his clothing was well alight. Using all his great strength, Thompson managed to lift Potts out of his turret, completely oblivious to the fact that his own clothing was now beginning to burn. Incredibly, Thompson put the unconscious Potts over his shoulder and began to walk back along the fuselage. One false move and both men could have fallen through the hole in the fuselage, yet Thompson carried on without a thought for his own safety and deposited the still burning Potts in a safer section of the fuselage. Once again without thinking, Thompson then proceeded to extinguish Potts burning clothing with his bare hands in an act that could only be driven by pure adrenalin.

This single act of bravery was remarkable in its own right and Thompson was himself in a terrible state, his clothing was shredded and his face and hands had been horribly burned. Having left Potts in the care of another crew member, Thompson then turned his attention to the rear-gunner, Sgt Price, whose turret was in the eye of the inferno. Price had already made one attempt to bail out after he received no response from his calls on the intercom. With no power to his turret, he

Flight Sergeant George Thompson VC, the bravest of wireless operators, who rescued both mid-upper and rear gunners from the burning fuselage of his 9 Squadron Lancaster.

A 9 Squadron pilot with his flight engineer by his side was typical of how close the working relationship was between these members of the aircrew.

manually rotated it so that the escape doors were clear of the rear fuselage, disconnected his heated flying suit, removed his flying helmet and opened the doors. At this point he must have thought he had opened the doors to hell, as the flames from the fire immediately poured into his turret, burning away the Welshman's hair in an instant and his ears with it. He quickly closed the doors and rotated his turret back to aft position, at which point, he heard a knock from outside. Price opened the doors and there stood the redoubtable George Thompson, even more singed and with even less of his uniform remaining; 'Come on out, Taffy,' was all he needed to say. Not in great shape himself, Price extricated himself from his cramped turret and, with Thompson's assistance, joined Potts, who was still unconscious and was being attended to by the navigator, Kneebone.

By this point a lesser man would most likely have slumped into unconsciousness but Thompson, who had already rescued two of his friends, was worried that Denton would give the order to bail out when neither of the two air gunners was in a fit state to do so. His face, hands and legs were black and blistering but this did not stop Thompson from going forward to tell his skipper about the plight of the two injured airmen.

Aided by Goebel and Hartshorn, Denton managed to keep PD368 on a westerly course, every mile flown bringing them closer to the Allied lines and safety. The crew's plight was not over yet and, as the bomber approached the Rhine, Goebel spotted a few puffs of flak bursting on the starboard side of the Lancaster. Denton instinctively started to take evasive action when the Lancaster was hit by yet another burst of flak. This time the starboard inner engine was knocked out. With the aircraft more balanced, Denton was at least able to release the pressure he had been applying on the rudder but by then, the bomber was down to 5,000 ft and would only fly so far on the two remaining engines. Denton held PD368 steady so that the absolute minimum rate of descent could be achieved, at which point, a formation of German fighters approached from ahead, appearing to bear down on the Lancaster. The crew of the Lancaster held their breath, only to watch their potentially lethal opponents completely ignore them and pass harmlessly overhead. They were, in fact, trying to out-run a determined bunch of Canadian Spitfire pilots who, on seeing the plight of the crippled Lancaster, decided to help.

'Jolly good landing, skipper'

Closing all around the descending Lancaster, the Spitfires attempted to steer it towards their own airfield but by then, the bomber was running out of altitude and it was time for Denton to put PD368 down. One of the fighter pilots accelerated ahead to indicate a line of high tension wires which Denton, with the last remnants of his strength, managed to coax the reluctant Lancaster over. It was then that he spotted the Dutch village of Vosbergstraat, south-west of Heesch, dead ahead. Denton managed to avoid it before turning the bomber towards a pair of large fields, split by a hedge-covered ridge. Lining up the Lancaster diagonally across the two fields, PD368 hit the ground more than halfway across the first field before sliding on its belly and careering through the hedge. The bomber split in two before coming to rest on the edge of the second field in a shower of shattered metal and covered in aviation fuel. Thankfully, there was no fire and all seven crew, including Potts, who had finally come around, extricated themselves from the wrecked aircraft.

It was only then, as the crew shook themselves down, that Denton realised that the airman who had come forward to tell him about the two injured air gunners was Thompson. His wireless operator was almost unrecognisable to him because of his charred condition and it was only when Thompson said, 'Jolly good landing, skipper', that Denton realised who he was. Denton instructed Goebel to go and get help in Heesch, while the skipper and Kneebone helped Thompson to a cottage close by. Hartshorn, who had also been burnt, assisted Price and Potts to the same cottage, whose occupants helped as best they could.

Back in the air, the enthusiastically helpful Spitfires had radioed ahead the crash position of the Lancaster to their home airfield and it was not long before a pair of military ambulances arrived. With the exception of Goebel, who was taken in by a local Allied army unit, Denton and his crew were delivered to Eindhoven Catholic hospital. Goebel was later transferred to the RAF Hospital at Rauceby where he was treated for severe frostbite which resulted in the loss of all of his fingers up to the first joint. Of the rest of the crew, the burning hydraulic fluid had taken its toll on Sgt Ernie Potts, who slumped back into unconsciousness whilst in the cottage, was destined not to recover. The air gunner from Newport, Monmouthshire passed away 18 hours later. Despite the severe burns he suffered around his head, rear gunner Sgt Price spent many months undergoing pioneering plastic surgery and went on to make a full recovery. The flight engineer, Hartshorn, was also sent to Rauceby where his burns were treated. He was back on duty within a few weeks.

After a spell in Eindhoven hospital, Thompson was transferred to the US 50th Military Field Hospital near Brussels where he responded very well to treatment. He was described as the perfect patient by the staff and at no time did he complain about his appalling injuries. Sadly, Thompson contracted pneumonia and passed away on 23 January 1945. The big man from Perthshire was laid to rest in Brussels Town Cemetery (X.27.45) and, on 16 February, it was announced in *The London Gazette* that he would be awarded a posthumous VC.

George Thompson's most deserved award, along with his campaign medals, is today on display in the National War Museum of Scotland in Edinburgh Castle and he is commemorated on the Portmoak Parish War Memorial located within the Bishopshire golf club at Portmoak.

Springbok Pathfinder

Edwin Swales, SAAF
(23/24 February 1945)

A willing volunteer

Our final recipient of the VC was not obliged to serve for any other country outside his own, but like so many of his countrymen from the First World War, he willingly volunteered to fight alongside similar-minded men from Britain and the Commonwealth.

One of four children, Edwin Essery Swales was born in Inanda, Natal, Union of South Africa, on 3 July 1915, the son of Harry Evelyn Swales and Olive Miriam Essery. A farmer who worked land in the Heatonville District, Harry succumbed to the post-First World War flu epidemic forcing Olive to move the family to Berea, Durban. Swales was educated at the Durban High School and after graduating in 1934 his first job was with the local branch of Barclays Bank. A very keen sportsman, he was particularly good at cricket, squash and rugby; at the latter he was good enough to play for Natal and several other South African and Dominion teams.

Swales' long military career began on 1 June 1935, when he joined the Natal Mounted Rifles (NMR), the equivalent of the British Territorials, and by May 1939 he had reached the rank of Warrant Officer II. After a brief spell back with Barclays, Swales was called up for full-time service with the NMR on 15 September 1939. On 9 June 1940, Swales volunteered for active service 'outside the Union' just as the NMR was declared fit for 'foreign service' under the new name of the 2nd South African Infantry Brigade. After some final training the unit was posted to Kenya, which was under threat of Italian invasion at the time, and then on to Southern

Abyssinia in February 1941 to meet the Italian forces head on. The brigade was then sent to North Africa, where it took part in two successful campaigns from El Alamein before it was withdrawn from action and sent back to South Africa.

SAAF transfer

Having taken part in every part of the 2nd South African Infantry Brigade's war to date, Swales decided he wanted to see action from a different aspect. On 17 January 1942 he volunteered to join the SAAF and after being accepted for pilot training, was sent to 75 Air School at Lyttleton, near Pretoria on 2 February. After this basic course he was posted to 4 Air School, Benoni on 8 October and on 29 October he made his first solo in a Tiger Moth. Conversion training followed in February 1943 at 21 Air School, Kimberley, where he was introduced to the twin-engine Oxford. On 26 June 1943 Swales gained his wings and was commissioned as Second Lieutenant in the SAAF.

In August 1943, he was given the option of remaining in South Africa for a further six months as an instructor, or joining the RAF on secondment with a subsequent operational tour of duty in the European Theatre of Operations. Swales chose the latter and on 21 August, along with 60 other volunteers from the SAAF, began the long journey to England, eventually arriving in November.

On 1 December he was posted to 6 (P)AFU at Little Rissington, equipped with the Anson and Oxford, where he was promoted to First Lieutenant. Swales was then posted to 83 OTU, Peplow, for conversion training on the Wellington which was completed in June 1944. After a short course at Warboys, Swales found himself being posted to 582 Squadron, a Pathfinder unit, at Little Staughton in early July 1944; his operational RAF career could now finally begin. On the squadron he was known as 'Ted', and after joining 'B' Flight, the South African pilot carried out his first practice flight in a Lancaster on 6 July. Six days later he flew his first operation, a daylight attack on Thivery on Lancaster PB149, '6O-D'.

The coming weeks saw an intensive period of operations with targets in northern France and Germany. Swales took part in the raid on Trossy-St-Maximin on 4 August, which saw the demise of Sqn Ldr Bazalgette; an operation in which the South African pilot's Lancaster suffered extensive flak damage but still managed to bomb the target and return home safely. Swales was transferred from 'B' to 'A' Flight, 582 Squadron and in early September 1944, his flying career nearly ended during a daylight operation to Duisburg on 14 October, in Lancaster PB963 '6O-J'. A victim of predicted flak, PB963 was in a delicate state with both port engines feathered, the starboard outer failing, and hydraulic lines severed, but Swales still managed to complete his bomb run and keep the aircraft in the air until he was

Captain Edwin Essery Swales, VC, DFC who was actually an 'acting' Major at the time of his death on 23 February 1945. His medals are on display at the South African National Museum of Military History, Saxonwold, Johannesburg while his miniatures are owned by his old school at Durban.

A nice snapshot (which were not then allowed to be taken!) by Harry Wright of 582 Squadron, showing a Lancaster and the night's bomb load being delivered at Little Staughton. The clutter and general disarray in the foreground was quite typical of all Bomber Command dispersals, much of the detritus and scrap metal was buried where it lay when the airfields were vacated during the post-war period.

forced to crash-land near Brussels. The crew were not injured and were flown to Little Staughton in an Anson. The following night he was back in the air again on a raid to Wilhelmshaven. On 4 November, he was promoted to Captain and was transferred back to 'B' Flight.

The four operations Swales flew during December 1944 were in the role of Deputy Master Bomber, including his 33rd operation to the Gremberg marshalling yards in Cologne. MB for this operation was Sqn Ldr R A M Palmer DFC. On seeing the demise of Palmer's Lancaster, Swales released his salvo of bombs before throwing his machine, like a fighter, out of the increasingly intensive sea of flak just as five German fighters jumped the Lancaster. Without fuss, Swales calmly swung from side to side so that his gunners were given the maximum opportunity to take on the enemy. The fighters attacked at least five times and during the engagement Swales' air gunners claimed one destroyed and two damaged. For this action Swales was awarded the DFC, part of the glowing citation saying, 'Throughout this spirited action Captain Swales displayed exceptional coolness and captaincy, setting a very fine example'. Swales' DFC was gazetted on 23 February 1945.

Master Bomber

The heavy responsibility of Master Bomber was bestowed upon Swales for the first time for a raid to Nuremberg on 2/3 January 1945. At the controls of Lancaster PB538, '6O-M', Swales remained in the air for almost seven hours and did not leave the target area until he was sure that all in the formation had bombed accurately. After further operations to Frankfurt, Ludwigshaven, Bonn and Goch, Swales was MB again for a raid on Chemnitz on 14/15 February. It was around this time that a paper trail had begun which would see Swales promoted to Major, but in the meantime all he could think about was the spell of well-deserved leave that he and his crew would take from 24 February. However, there was still time for one more raid, and once again Swales would act as Master Bomber.

Target Pforzheim

The target for the night of 23/24 February was the town of Pforzheim, the location of an important railway junction between Karlsruhe and Stuttgart. This railway was an important German supply line feeding the units fighting against the US 7th Army. It was vital that it was destroyed, and the town, which had never been attacked before, would undoubtedly suffer.

For this operation Swales would fly his regular Lancaster PB538, '6O-M' along with his usual highly experienced crew. These were Sqn Ldr D P D Archer DSO, DFC

'Ted' Swales and his crew at Little Staughton on the morning of 23 February 1945. (In front of Swales) Dodson; (left to right standing) Archer, Bennington and Wheaton RAAF; (left to right front row) Leach, Bourne RCAF and Goodacre RAAF.

(navigator); Plt Off R A Wheaton RAAF (second navigator); Flt Lt C Dodson DSO, DFC (bomb aimer); Plt Off A V Goodacre RAAF (wireless operator); Flt Sgt B Leach (mid-upper gunner); Plt Off N Bourne RCAF (rear gunner); and Flt Sgt G Bennington (flight engineer) who had flown 34 operations with Swales.

After taking off from Little Staughton at 1636 hrs, Swales had an uneventful outward flight until he arrived over the target. Just eight minutes after dropping his target indicators and while still controlling the raid, Swales' Lancaster was attacked by an Me410 flown by Hptm G Friedrich of II/NJG1. The fighter was seen first by Bourne, the rear gunner, who lost sight of it before spotting it climbing towards PB538 to attack again. Bourne called for Swales to dive to starboard, but the message never got through and the Me410 opened fire at 800 yds while the rear gunner returned fire. Bourne saw his tracer hit the night-fighter but Friedrich continued his attack, raking the Lancaster with long bursts of fire. By now, the mid-upper gunner, Leach, also picked up the fighter at 400 yds but could not get a bead on until it broke away to port. Leach also scored hits on the Me410 as the fighter rolled off the top of its turn and dived away vertically.

The attack had taken its toll on the Lancaster. The tail plane and rudder were damaged and the port inner engine was in flames, although the fire came under control when the engine was feathered. The starboard inner also had to be feathered, and the starboard fuel tank was holed. Swales ordered his crew to don their parachutes but rescinded the order when he realised that PB538 continued to perform as normal and even dared to climb. The main concern was how long the electrics would last because the generator was driven off the inner engines and, without current, the crucial DR compass would fail. Approaching a cold front, the loss of blind-flying instruments put the aircraft in perilous danger and, once again, the captain ordered his crew to don parachutes and bail out. When the last crewman was safely out of the Lancaster, Swales tried to make a crash-landing but, as he descended, he struck some high-tension cables and spun into the ground at Chappelle-aux-Bois, south of Valenciennes.

Pforzheim was almost wiped off the map in that one raid by 367 Lancasters and 13 Mosquitoes from 1, 6 and 8 Groups. The main force approached the target at just 5,000 ft until it reached 07°00 E over Saarbrücken and then climbed to 8,000 ft, on track for Pforzheim. Despite the spoofing (including a Mandrel Screen and Window) and the different approach to the target, a large formation of enemy night fighters was already congregating over Stuttgart and they would make their presence felt. Ten Lancasters were shot down and two more crashed in France, including that of MB, Major Swales.

Pforzheim was an example of one of the most concentrated RAF raids of the war. It was an accurate aerial bombing which saw 1,825 tons of bombs fall within

22 minutes, devastating over 80 per cent of the town. It is believed that 17,600 people were killed, the majority in a firestorm which erased a large area of the town. The death toll was only surpassed by Hamburg and Dresden during the entire war.

The crew of Swales' aircraft all survived their rapid exit from the doomed Lancaster but they had a grim discovery when they visited the crash site the next morning. 'Ted' Swales was inside the shattered cockpit of the bomber, his hands still firmly clasped around the control column. The determined South African had done his duty to the bitter end.

For his actions that day, Major E E Swales was awarded Bomber Command's last, and 8 Group's third VC of the war. Part of his citation, which was gazetted on 24 April 1945 read, 'Intrepid in attack, courageous in the face of danger, he did his duty to the last, giving his life that his comrades might live.' Major Swales VC was laid to rest in the Leopoldsburg War Cemetery (VIII. C.5.).

Appendix

Blockbuster   4,000, 8,000 or 12,000 lb high capacity blast bomb

Cookie   4,000 lb high capacity blast bomb

Gardening   Mine laying operations

H2S   Radar aid for navigation and target identification

Mandrel   Airborne radar jamming device 85-135 MHz to counter the German Freya early warning system

Master Bomber   A single, controlling commander of an entire bombing operation who made sure that markers were positioned correctly and the appropriate aircraft bombed on them at the correct time.

Nickel   Raid involving the dropping of propaganda or warning leaflets.

Oboe   *Oboe* was the codename given to the ground-controlled blind bombing device which was incredibly accurate for the day. The device could operate at heights up to 30,000 ft and speeds in excess of 300 mph but could still achieve an operational error of just 300 yards. This distance reduced dramatically at lower altitudes.

Pathfinder Force   Elite RAF squadrons whose purpose was to locate and mark bomb targets with a flame that the bombing crews following behind could aim at. They changed the fortunes of Bomber Command by increasing the accuracy of the bombing campaigns.

Spoofing　　　　A separate, diversionary attack, which grew in size as the war progressed, designed to draw enemy forces away from the main attack.

Vic Formation　　A formation of three aircraft, one in the lead with two others positioned either side and slightly to the rear.

Window　　　　　Strips of metallised paper, cut to a specific length and dropped in bundles to produce spurious responses on the enemies' radar screens. First use delayed until July 24/25 1943 over Hamburg.

Abbreviations

AASF	Advanced Air Strike Force
ACM	Air Chief Marshal
ADC	Aide-de-Camp
AI	Airborne Interception
AOS	Air Observers School
AST	Air Service Training
ATS	Armament Training Station
BEF	British Expeditionary Forces
BFTS	British Flying Training School
BG	Bomb Group
BGS	Bombing & Gunnery School
CAS	Chief of the Air Staff
CF	Conversion Flight
CGM	Conspicuous Gallantry Medal
CMG	Companions of the Order of St Michael and St George
CO	Commanding Officer
CWGC	Commonwealth War Graves Commission
DFC	Distinguished Flying Cross

DFM	Distinguished Flying Medal
DR	Dead Reckoning
EATS	Empire Air Training Scheme
EFTS	Elementary Flying Training School
E&RFTS	Elementary & Reserve Flying Training School
Flt Lt	Flight Lieutenant
Flt Lt (A)	Flight Lieutenant (Acting)
FO	Flying Officer
FTS	Flying Training School
HC	High Capacity
HCU	Heavy Conversion Unit
Hptm	Hauptmann (German Captain)
H/T	High Tension
IFF	Identification friend or foe
ITS	Initial Training School
ITW	Initial Training Wing
IWM	Imperial War Museum
JG	*Jagdgeschwader* (equal to an RAF Wing)
LAC	Leading Aircraftsman
LDV	Local Defence Volunteers
LNSF	Light Night Striking Force
MA	Master of Arts
MB	Master Bomber
Mjr	Major
MP	Member of Parliament
NZPAF	New Zealand Permanent Air Force

ORB	Operations Record Book
OTU	Operational Training Unit
(P)AFU	(Pilots) Advanced Flying Unit
PDC	Personnel Despatch Centre
PFF	Pathfinder Force
Plt Off	Pilot Officer
PRC	Personnel Reception Centre
PRO	Public Relations Officer
RAAF	Royal Australian Air Force
RAFVR	Royal Air Force Volunteer Reserve
RLG	Relief Landing Ground
RNZAF	Royal New Zealand Air Force
SAAF	South African Air Force
SFTS	Service Flying Training School
SOC	Struck Off Charge
SQN LDR	Squadron Leader
UAS	University Air Squadron
Uffz	Unteroffizier (Under Officer)
VC	Victoria Cross
Wg Cdr	Wing Commander
W/O	Warrant Officer
WOP/AG	Wireless Operator/Air Gunner
W/T	Wireless Transmitter

Bibliography

2 Group 1936-45, M J F Bowyer, Faber

Air 27/128/20, 9 Squadron (LM548), National Archives

Air 27/129/1, 2, 9 Squadron, National Archives

Air 27/164/17, 12 Squadron, National Archives

Air 27/578/17, 19, 21, 61 Squadron, National Archives

Air 27/645, 75(NZ) Squadron, National Archives

Air 27/834/7, 8, 106 Squadron, National Archives

Air 27/1002/22, 149 Squadron, National Archives

Air 27/1823/8, 9, 12, 13, 419 Squadron, National Archives

Air 27/1935/14, 487 Squadron, National Archives

Air 27/2050, 578 Squadron, National Archives

Air 28/681, RAF Scampton, National Archives

Air 50/270/2, 487 Squadron, National Archives

Bomber Squadrons of the RAF, Macdonald, P Moyes

For Valour – The Air VCs, C Bowyer, Caxton

RAF Flying Training & Support, R Sturtivant/J Hamlin, Air Britain

RAF Bomber Command Losses 1939-40, W R Chorley, Midland Counties

RAF Bomber Command Losses 1941, W R Chorley, Midland Counties

RAF Bomber Command Losses 1942, W R Chorley, Midland Counties

RAF Bomber Command Losses 1943, W R Chorley, Midland Counties

RAF Flying Training & Support, R Sturtivant & J Hamlin, Air Britain

RAF Squadrons, C G Jefford, Airlife

The Bomber Command War Diaries, M Middlebrook & C Everitt, Midland Counties

The Fairey Battle, S Shail, Air Britain

The Stirling Story, M J F Bowyer, Crécy

WO 98/8, Barton VC, National Archives

Index

UNITS

Luftwaffe

RAF Squadrons

106 26, 64, 65, 94-95, 130
107 34-35, 86
109 158-160
114 78
115 150, 152
122 86-87
139 33
149 71-73, 152, 156
156 71, 158
185 51
207 51, 53, 94
214 89
218 102-103, 106
419 137, 138
420 63
453 86, 87
460 38
487 84-86
578 122
582 158, 161-162, 172, 174-175
614 78, 81
617 68, 95, 100, 117-118, 145, 146
627 100, 130
630 100
635 152-154

RAF Miscellaneous Units

1 Group 130, 178
2 E&WTS 25
2 FTS 8
2 Group 55, 84, 86
2 SoAN 62
2 SS 32

3 ATS 92
3 E&RFTS 16
3 FTS 8
3 ITW 156
4 B&GS 26
5 Group 53, 74, 92-95, 97-98, 130, 147, 166
6 Group 178
6 FTS 92
6 Group 137, 140
6 (P)AFU 102, 112, 120,
7 EFTS 156
7 ITW 112
8 E&RFTS 51
8 Group 71, 103, 130, 152, 154-155, 158, 160-161, 178
9 FTS 46, 141
10 OTU 142
11 FTS 16, 51
12 FTS 51, 156
14 OTU 24, 32, 53, 62, 93, 163
15 OTU 156
16 OTU 26, 93, 137
17 OTU 84
19 OTU 120
20 OTU 40, 152, 156, 158
23 OTU 69
25 OTU 24, 62, 150
26 OTU 102
26 CF 71
27 MU 64
27 OTU 130
29 OTU 112

44 CF 61
51 OTU 94
54 Base HQ 100
55 Base HQ 100
83 OTU 172
106 CF 65
107 OTU 24
109 OTU 24
326 Wing 78, 80
1314 Flt 24
1651 HCU 61, 71
1652 HCU 144
1654 HCU 112, 130, 163
1657 HCU 102
1661 HCU 137
1663 HCU 121
1664 HCU 137

Commonwealth Miscellaneous Units

1 (British) FTS (Terrel) 102
1 EFTS (Taieri) 40
2 BFTS (War Eagle) 112
2 ITS (Bradfield Park) 69
2 Wireless School (Calgary) 136
3 B&GS (Macdonald) 136
4 Air School (Benoni) 174
5 EFTS (Narromine) 69
21 Air School (Kimberley) 174
38 SFTS (Monckton) 112
75 Air School (Lyttleton) 172
Levin ITW 39